SEARCHING FOR HOME

*-a personal journey of transformation
and healing after a near-death experience*

Dedication

**To the loving Light
and spirit guides,**
Elijah and Methuselah
for showing me the way home.

To my sister
Gwendolyn G. Carbone,
my best friend,
for your faith in my writing ability,
your meticulous editorial skills and for
exemplifying that love at the soul level exists.

To my mother
Barbara L. Glass,
my guardian angel,
for your guidance, encouragement and
unconditional love during my life's journey.

To my husband
Byron E. Martin,
my soul connection,
for sharing your radiant light and love.

To my son
Elijah Evans Martin,
my miracle child,
for showing me
that anything is possible.

SEARCHING FOR HOME

-a personal journey of transformation
and healing after a near-death experience

Laurelynn G. Martin

Cosmic
Concepts

2531 Dover Lane
St. Joseph, Michigan 49085

SEARCHING FOR HOME
-a personal journey of transformation
and healing after a near-death experience   © Laurelynn G.Martin - 1996

Library of Congress Cataloging-in-Publication Data

Martin, Laurelynn G., 1961-
        Searching for home : a personal journey of transformation and
healing after a near-death experience / Laurelynn G. Martin
        p.   cm.
    ISBN 0-9620507-5-x
        1.   Near-death experiences. 2. Martin, Laurelynn G., 1961-
I. Title.
BF1045.N4M37   1996
133.9'01'3--dc20   96-21539
                          CIP

Published by COSMIC CONCEPTS
2531 Dover Lane, St. Joseph, MI 49085

printed and bound in the United States of America

10 9 8 7 6 5 4 3 2 1

Preface

As I began writing, I wondered how to convey my experiences on paper. The challenge to phrase words and thoughts for a universal appeal had my analytical, logical mind concerned. Yet, I knew, this wasn't a book to be scrutinized with logic for the words that resonated in my head were: "Write from your heart... Everything will be understood... For love is a universal language." My heart, with all its tender vulnerabilities, I present to you.

I have learned that one moment, one insight, one word, one vision or one experience can change one's life. I have also learned there are no magic formulas to find meaning in life. What we do with our experiences gives us meaning and transformation.

Therefore, I have written about my experience - my personal journey, not because it's anything special, for many of you have overcome far greater obstacles than I. Yet, any obstacle, however great or small, is noteworthy. I write about my story to encourage and inspire you to continue your efforts and share your story with others. All the stories I have heard or read have given me hope, inspiration and love. In some small way, I hope my writing does the same.

I was at the height of a promising tennis career, when I had a routine surgical procedure that catastrophically sent me into an ecstatic world of light,
beauty and love on the "other side." I was Home - Home in the Light!

Upon my reluctant return, I became a chronic pain patient, taking thirty-six prescription pills a day, relentlessly searching for that place called Home. After twelve years of medical complications and reparative surgeries, I overcame, what Western medical doctors labeled, an "incurable" condition. A combination of alternative therapies, allopathic medicine, faith healing in the Philippines, spiritual guidance from the other side, alignment with my true spiritual nature, and hope and love have given me health and wellness today.

I have found home within myself and from outside support. My husband, my family and people like you, who continue to meet the challenges of being human, are part of my homecoming. I have watched how many of you have overcome struggle and continue to find the positive aspects of living. I have learned to live life in the moment, in the here and now, because that's all there is. And home is not a place to go to, but an idea to be lived, every moment of every day.

Thank you for embarking upon this journey. Thank you for opening your heart, for when we are both in that place as "one," we are home.

L.G.M.

Table of Contents

PART I
A Personal Journey

PART II
Universal Messages

PART I: A Personal Journey

Chapter 1

No Vacancy

The future enters into us,
in order to transform itself in us,
long before it happens.

-Rainer Maria Rilke

On a gray, metallic stretcher bed, I waited in a dimly lit hallway outside the operating room. Feeling half-naked with the blue floral cotton johnny tied loosely around my back, I wondered how long I would have to wait. Feeling the cool, clear plastic intravenous tubing against my wrist, and a draft of foul smelling air gape open my gown, I clutched the thin material closer to my breasts. What an inconvenience to delay my final college exams to have this operation. But I needed to have a laparoscopic exploratory surgical procedure to find out why I had stopped menses for eight months. All I wanted at this moment was a bit of warmth on this cold December day in northeast Connecticut.

"Could I have a blanket, please?" I asked a redheaded nurse scurrying by. "Make that two," I said, as if the soft white barrier of blankets would protect me.

A few minutes later a nurse returned. "I found some heated blankets for you," she said.

"How did you know I wanted blankets?" I boldly asked.

"You just asked me."

"You don't look like the same nurse. She had red hair."

She chuckled, pulled out a lock of hair from under what looked like a shower cap and said, "It's me. See."

She paused, with an air of amusement. "You've never had surgery before, have you?"

I shook my head no.

"I didn't think so," she replied with a knowing grin. "It won't be much longer before we're ready for you. Try to relax."

Curled under the minuscule warmth of the heated flannel blankets, my stomach fluttered nervously like a fishing bobber at the end of a pole. It reminded me of waiting on the sidelines of a tennis court before the big match - anxious apprehension of an unknown event. I never knew what to expect. Sometimes there was too much wind, too many sock wrinkles under a foot arch, or the opponent was tougher than anticipated.

"Always anticipate the unexpected," my tennis coach would say. I never quite understood how that was possible. How could you know what you didn't know? My approach was to get on the court and finish the game. I never thought about upcoming events because then a million "what if's" could go wrong.

As I moved to reposition my cold torso away from the hard metal slats, I brought one arm up and cradled my head. My thoughts comforted me as I drifted to the past, not to the upcoming, impending event...

At age twenty-one, I was on top of the world - a healthy, senior college athlete. I was seeded #1 in doubles on the women's tennis team and #3 in the singles position. I loved competition. I loved training four hours each weekday and ten to twelve hours on the weekends. I loved pushing my body physically and mentally to its limits and feeling an exhilaration beyond words when I reached that place of sheer exhaustion - aching muscles, heavy breathing - yet feeling in the best shape of my life. I didn't know at that time that I was also pushing myself to my emotional and spiritual limits.

My spiritual life was the typical religious routine of Sunday school until about eighth grade. At age twelve, I was old enough to voice my opinion and told my parents, "I'd rather be outside playing ball." My emotional life was that of a hardened athlete. Training included enduring hardship and tolerating pain. Expressing sadness or tears didn't make good athletes. "It was a weakness," I was told. Growing up with three brothers also encouraged this way of thinking: "Crybabies" couldn't play sports, yet expressing anger on the ball field made you a hero.

With my imbalances in all realms of living, it's a wonder I found myself surprised when I stopped menstruating for eight consecutive months. As I've since learned, my body has a phenomenal way of telling me when it needs attention. However, in the spring of my junior year in college, I was focused on athletics and didn't pay attention to anything else. I didn't notice my brother-in-law's plight. At age thirty, he was dying of cancer. Again, I found myself surprised when my older sister, Gwen, called. "John has just been admitted to Massachusetts General Hospital. It doesn't look good. I don't know if he's going to make it," she told me with controlled emotion.

Her husband, John Williams, whom I affectionately called "Wills" was about to die. I was stunned. He passed over at week's end. I wish I had spent more time with him. He was such a kind man. It all seemed so sudden.

My brother-in-law fit into my family like a blood relation. We were a close, caring group. My parents had six children within an eight year span. Three boys and three girls, "The Brady Bunch," as we were often teased. I was the middle daughter, with brothers on either side of the hierarchical birth order. Although we had our share of fights growing up, the older we became the less sibling rivalry we had, leading to a genuine love and concern for each other. With so many children, attention rarely came my way. I didn't mind. I figured I'd been given an opportunity to be self-sufficient. I depended on myself and decided at a young age if I was to be noticed, I would become the best I could be. The arena I chose was athletics.

I was always striving, achieving and performing, from sixth grade basketball star to high school class athlete to collegiate amateur. I was offered a choice to play basketball or tennis on a college scholarship. A professional tennis athlete had greater opportunities than a female basketball player. So, I chose tennis and went to Indiana State University, a division one school. I was striving for career potential.

Even in the face of family tragedy, my self-absorption continued and to some degree increased. "Wills" passed away and I felt more driven than ever to achieve my goals. After all, death could come and blow all your plans. I must hurry before time ran out.

That summer, I spent two weeks with Gwen while she was grieving. Emotions weren't a comfortable place to be, so I became a Rotary International exchange student touring Europe and playing tennis. I still wasn't menstruating but I didn't mind. I was relieved of what I had always considered an inconvenience. However, I wanted to remain healthy and fit so I could play at the National Tennis Tournament next spring with my doubles partner and continue on to the women's professional tennis circuit after graduation. All my striving to succeed was nearing the ultimate reward. The status of becoming a professional athlete, something I had always dreamed of, was about to come true.

In the fall, I returned for my senior year in college. My menstrual cycles remained abnormal. I had read somewhere that low body fat in highly trained athletes as well as undue amounts of psychological stress, could stop menstruation. What stress could I possibly be under? Normal college stress, or maybe the pressure of competition, but that was the kind of pressure I thrived on or was it? The death of my brother-in-law was a stressful event but that was seven months ago. I decided to follow the advice of my mother's gynecologist and have a laparoscopy, a minor surgical procedure to view the abdominal cavity. I scheduled the procedure in December so I could finish the fall tennis season. I could rest during Christmas break and return to school in January to train for the National Tennis Tournament. But that was not meant to be.

Chapter 2

Home in the Light

To die will be an awfully big adventure.

-James M. Barrie, (*Peter Pan*)

"Are you sleeping?"

I heard a muffled voice and looked up. The same nurse was in a new disguise. Now she had a white corrugated gauze-type mask over her nose and mouth.

"I'm just thinking," I said shyly with a half-smile as I lowered my arm to get a firmer grasp on my gown. "Is it my turn to go in?"

"Yes, we're ready for you," she replied. As I was wheeled into the sterile, austere looking operating room, the nurse continued to chat, to ease my worries. "The procedure will only take about twenty minutes. You can go home about two hours later."

She helped me slide onto the operating table and gave me a motherly look. "Don't worry. We know it's your first time. We'll make this a most pleasant experience for you."

With those reassuring words, I drifted off to sleep. I awakened and found myself floating above my body, off to the right side, looking down, watching the attempts of the medical team trying to revive the lifeless form below. I viewed the scene with detachment. The surgical team was frantic. The color red was everywhere, splattered on their gowns, splattered on the floor, and a bright pool of a flowing red substance, in the now wide open abdominal cavity. At that moment, I didn't make the connection, that the body being worked on was my own! It didn't matter anyway. I was in a state of floating freedom, experiencing no pain and having a great time. I wanted to shout to the distressed people below, "Hey, I'm okay. It's fantastic up here," but they were so intent on their work, I didn't want to interrupt their efforts.

I had traveled to another realm of total and absolute peace. With no physical body my movement was unencumbered. Thought was the avenue for travel. I floated up through blackness where there was no fear, no pain, no misunderstandings, but instead a sense of well-being. I was enveloped by total bliss in an atmosphere of unconditional love and acceptance. The darkness was warm and soft, a blanket of velvety love, stretching endlessly. The freedom of total peace was intensified beyond any ecstatic feeling I've ever felt on earth. In the distance, a horizon of glorious white, golden light beckoned me forward.

As the brilliance increased and the encompassing rays stretched to meet me, I felt that time, as we know it, was nonexistent. Time and existence were a blending and a melding of the past, present and future into this one moment. A sense of all-knowing enveloped me. Every part of my being was satisfied, with an unconditional love beyond description. All questions were answered. An inner peace without striving or achieving was created and understood.

It flashed in my mind, this was the pleasant experience the nurse had spoken about. I understood why she didn't elaborate. Words and descriptions somehow lost the essence of the experience.

As I admired the beauty of the light, I was drawn closer, feeling the radiant warmth, infinite love and lasting peace. I felt as if I were home - home in the light. Before I became further engulfed in the light, I became aware of many spirits. They surrounded, embraced and supported my journey with their gentleness, knowledge and guidance. I felt one of them approach from my right upper side. This familiar presence came forward and my feelings changed to sheer joy when I discovered my thirty year old brother-in-law, the one who had died seven months earlier from cancer. My essence moved to meet his essence.

I couldn't see with my eyes or hear with my ears, yet I instinctively knew that it was "Wills." I heard his smile, saw his laughter and felt his humor. It didn't make sense, but it made complete sense. We were separate but we were also one. It was as if I had come home and my brother-in-law was here to greet me. I instantly thought how glad I was to be with him, because now I could make up for the last time I had seen him before his death. I felt sad and a bit guilty for not taking the time out of my busy schedule to have a heart-to-heart talk with him when he had asked me to. I realized I was not being judged by him but by myself. I was in his position - dying, wanting to say goodbye to those I loved, and then meeting people like myself not "getting it"- not getting that all the achievement, money or recognition in the world cannot be taken with you when you die. The only thing you take with you is the love you give away.

Wills gave love away his whole life. In a sense he was ready to leave our physical world and continue his work in the spiritual world. People, like my sister, who were left behind without their beloved, sometimes didn't understand. I would have to remember to tell Gwen about my discovery.

The ones who depart are in a loving space with much guidance, understanding and purpose. Their wish upon departure is not to bring sorrow and grief to others but to honor the divine plan. It is their time for transition, for the continued development of their soul. Many times, the departed loved one will work in ways to help, serve and guide others.

Wills' gentle guidance allowed me to view my innocence. I understood, instantly, life was about people not pursuits. I was putting pursuits first as a means to seek approval and love from people. Once I understood, I forgave myself for my actions and in the act of **forgiving** I received love in abundance.

By giving love, one receives and experiences a tremendous love from the universe.

Wills was like the "Spirit of Christmas Past." By reviewing my past, I was brought to new places of discovery within myself. Many events were shown simultaneously. I recalled two examples. When I was five years old I teased Tammy Fowler, another five year old girl, to the point of tears. I was now in a unique position to feel what Tammy felt. Her frustration, her tears, and her feelings of separateness were now my feelings. I felt a tremendous amount of compassion for this child. I was Tammy and needed love, nurturing and forgiveness. My essence gave love to both of us - a love so deep and tender, like the love between a mother and child. I realized by hurting another, I was only hurting myself. Again, I was experiencing oneness.

The next incident was similar. I had made fun of Billy Bradley, a scrawny, malnourished asthmatic kid. He died when he was seventeen years old from a cerebral aneurysm. He seemed to be in the same plane of existence I was in. Yet, still I was not sure where I was. When Billy was twelve, he had written me a love letter that I rejected. I was experiencing his pain which became my pain. At the same time, I felt a tremendous amount of love for this boy and myself. My contact with him went beyond the physical and I felt his soul. He had a vibrant, bright light burning inside of him. Feeling his spirit's strength and vitality was an inconceivable moment especially knowing how much he physically suffered when he was alive.

The message was clear. The message was - **LOVE**.

Above and beyond anything else, one must first learn to love oneself non-judgmentally and unconditionally. Then one will actually love all people and all things the same way.

I realized how important people were in life, how important it was to accept them and love them. And I finally understood the old Mohegan Indian saying I had heard when I was in Girl Scouts, "Never judge another squaw until you have walked a mile in her moccasins."

As I reviewed my life with Wills, my judgment prevailed and I remember thinking, "I've done worse things in my life." My question was answered before I finished my thought.

All events in your life are significant. To bring an understanding to all things, even the experiences which you consider insignificant, will bring you to places of great awareness and compassion.

By the time my review was finished, I understood. I was aware of an almost cathartic release. I experienced emotion without the physical signs of tears. It brought me to a deep place of understanding and compassion. I never took the time to think how my actions affected others or how I treated myself. I felt a grieving for all my unconscious actions. With awareness of my unaware state, I released all the grief I had ever caused and joyfully moved into forgiveness.

Other thoughts were conveyed and I remember thinking, "Wow, now I get it. Everything about our existence finally makes sense." I had more questions for Wills. The transference of information was immense and reassuring. He kept saying, "All is known. You have simply forgotten."

I didn't feel like I knew anything; yet, there was a place in me that knew everything. I asked Wills if I could stay. He said, "It's not your time yet. There's been a mistake. You have to go back."

I remember thinking, "Okay, I'll go back, but I can get back up here."

At that same instant his thoughts were mine, "You can't take your own life. Suicide, for you, isn't the answer. That won't do it. You have to go back and live your life's purpose."

I responded, "I understand, but I don't want to go back."

Wills' thought came to me again, "It's okay. We're not going anywhere. We'll be here for you again." His last communication was, "Tell your sister, I'm fine."

With those final thoughts, I felt myself going back, dropping downward through darkness. I was not afraid. Instantly, I felt myself slam into my body. My head was turned to the left and my right foot was intensely cold. At that point, I felt the most incredible searing pain imaginable in my abdomen, all the way through to my back bone. I couldn't breathe on my own. A big plastic pipe was stuck in my throat. Every time it moved, I was forced to puff. I felt as if my insides were popping. I couldn't believe I was returned to such a hellish environment, but then the beauty of the experience flooded back to me. I wavered in between the serene effects of the light I had just experienced and the excruciating pain that grew more intense with each breath.

Chapter 3

Distant Voices

For the meaning of life differs from man to man,
from day to day and from hour to hour.
What matters, therefore, is not the meaning of life in general
but rather the specific meaning of a person's life at a given moment.

- Victor Frankl

I tried to awaken but found I was struggling to hold onto consciousness. I knew something wasn't right. I knew this was more than the twenty minute surgical procedure the nurse had told me about. I could barely move without feeling a stabbing pain in my abdomen and back. I felt a tube at my nose, a corrugated plastic tug at my throat and burning urine from my vagina dribble into a bag pressed against my leg.

A tall male figure in a white coat spoke to me. I didn't recognize him, but I listened closely.

"I'm Dr. Samms. I took over your case from Dr. Epsom. He was really shaken last night."

Why was Dr. Epsom shaken? I wondered. Was he hurt? Did something happen to him too? I didn't understand. Why was I still in the hospital? I wished I could speak.

Dr. Samms continued, "He had to exert more than normal force to make the initial incision. With the extra force applied, the abdominal aorta was punctured. It's the largest blood vessel in the body. You also received injuries to your right iliac artery, the inferior vena cava, and two places in the bowel were punctured. The vertebral spine was also hit."

He saw my confused look and continued, "You had no blood coming away from your heart and no blood going back to your heart. You had no pulse. You lost three and a half liters of blood (the body only has five to six liters). Massive blood transfusions were needed."

My look of glazed confusion turned to disbelief. No pulse? That meant I was dead - how could that be? I wasn't in any danger. I was in a comfortable, loving space until I awoke to find this man standing over me.

His next words jolted me. "I snatched you from the jaws of death. Your chances of living were slim to none."

I was so tired. He didn't understand where I had been. I wasn't in the land of the dead. Everything and everyone was very much alive, just in different ways than what we know here.

"We had to open you all the way up so you're going to be sore. You're not out of the woods yet, so I need you to keep breathing and keep concentrating."

That was a lot to ask. I just wanted to go "home" - home to that peaceful place I had just returned from.

Through the fog of morphine shots, given every two to three hours, the details were slowly making sense. I learned that Dr. Samms was new in town. He recently moved here from Texas where he specialized in gun shot and stab wounds at Parkland City Hospital. He was walking by my surgical suite, when the emergency call went out. He ran into the operating room, performed an emergency exploratory laparotomy. He reached into my abdominal cavity and grabbed the aorta to close off the blood flow from further leakage. He proceeded to take all the abdominal contents out of the cavity, place them on a table next to my body, and sponge out the entire cavity. He said he examined all the vessels and organs for damage. Also, there wasn't enough blood in the surgical area and an emergency call for unscreened blood went out to the rest of the hospital.

After five hours of reparative surgery, I was taken to the recovery room in critical condition. I couldn't talk because I was on life support systems but the piercing abdominal pain and the intense coldness in my right foot got my attention. I now knew what "chilled to the bone" meant. I gestured toward my foot with my right arm because my left arm was swollen and bruised. The nurse informed me later my arm was swollen from phlebitis. A man with a dark brown mustache in green garb kept stroking my face saying, "You're going to be all right, you're going to be all right."

I kept shaking my head no and pointed to my right leg. I was definitely sent back for a reason, and the first reason was to save my own life by alerting the medical team of this new event.

I had developed a right femoral artery blood clot in my leg. I had to go in for three more hours of surgery. I was brought to the Intensive Care Unit (ICU) in critical condition, after eight hours of surgery, where my parents, younger sister, Ginger, and the family minister were waiting in despair. The next forty-eight to seventy-two hours were critical to see if I would live.

Every five minutes on the hour an attractive couple floated gracefully into my room. The man was dressed in a black business suit and had a disturbed but determined look on his face. The attractive woman had thick, wavy, salt and pepper hair. She came over and held my hand whispering kind, loving words. I figured out later that they were my parents, whom I had never appreciated so much in my life until that moment.

I couldn't wait to tell someone what had happened to me. I wanted to share this beautiful experience. The next day, my father spoke to me and said, "No more operations, Honey. We just want you to come home."

I tried to speak but I was on a respirator. My father noticed I wanted to communicate so he had one of the nurses get him a board and a piece of paper. I tried writing about what happened but I was very weak and nothing made sense. The only words that I legibly wrote were "They got me." I wanted to expand upon that thought and explain to him - Heaven had me, the light had me and I was fine, but everything was now being misunderstood. He thought I meant the doctors and the medical team "got me or injured me." And I wanted to tell him that he couldn't possibly take me home because I had already been home - home in the "Light" - a peaceful, painless state of existence. I wanted to share the depths of my feelings with everyone.

The initial reaction from my family was, "We just want you to get better. There's plenty of time to talk later. Just be quiet now and rest."

The health care professionals shrugged off my ramblings and said, "You're highly medicated."

I tried one more time to reach the beyond when I was being weaned off the respirator. The nurse instructed me to breathe on my own. She firmly warned, "If you stop breathing, the alarm will go off. You must concentrate."

I heard a deafening buzzing noise. I thought, "I must not be breathing. Great, I can go now."

I felt myself drift out of my body and this time, I was actually being sucked away. I was in a tube of darkness, traveling at "warp" speed. At one end was the ICU room and at the other end was the loving, golden light. As I looked back at the ICU - the figures became small and the voices, distant. Wills' words came to me - "It's not your time yet. We'll be here for you again."

I heard a barely audible whisper turn into a demanding command, "Come on, you can breathe on your own. You were doing it before. Let's go! We're waiting."

I was reminded of my old tennis coach, Doris Brientenfeld, cheering me on. The athlete in me had always liked a challenge. If I wanted to survive, I could. Next, I heard my mother's voice, "Honey, just keep trying."

I had forgotten my mother was in the room with me. She must be worried. With the thought of my mother, I returned. I felt myself enter my painful body. My breathing was shallow but sufficient. I talked to myself as if I was outside watching. It helped to keep distance from the pain and trauma. I kept saying, "Okay Laur, If you want to live, you have to keep breathing."

This one operation changed my life forever. I'd never be that young woman whose hopes and dreams were that of a professional athlete. The course of events that transpired set into motion a much deeper awareness and understanding of not only myself but of humanity and our planet. The conscious **process** of living suddenly became very important - not the **outcome**!

Chapter 4

Lingering Light

What though the radiance
which was once so bright
Be now forever taken from my sight,
Though nothing can bring back the hour
Of splendor in the grass,
Of glory in the flower;
We will grieve not, rather find
Strength in what remains behind;

-William Wordsworth

After experiencing the other side, I came back loving everything and everyone. I was no longer concerned with materialism. But I was angry to return to a world that didn't understand the importance of living life to its fullest, every minute of every day. "Live life consciously in the moment" was my motto, for one never knows when it will be time to go to the next world. This new motto of mine had one downfall. It didn't lend to planning ahead. I never expected to live beyond the next day. Planning for a future was absurd.

According to most doctors, operations take six to eight weeks to recover. Since my body was strong going into the operation, I thought I would be swinging a racket in no time. Two things stopped me. The first obstacle was my physical condition. I formed keloid or hypertrophic scars. A hypertrophic scar, an inherited condition from my family, is one that continues to grow abnormally. The external scar is usually raised, red and tender to the touch. The internal scarring, called adhesions, also grows abnormally and a sticky cobweb like substance is formed.

Every organ and every intestine that was handled during the first surgery formed adhesions. Structures began adhering to the front and back of the abdominal cavity and stuck to each other. I had no idea that the act of removing all my abdominal organs to save my life would actually be the biggest challenge to continue my existence. I was working on short-term rehabilitation. I never thought this condition would continue to plague me for another twelve years.

Secondly, my values and belief system had changed. What used to be important was no longer important. Materialism, success, social status, competitiveness and achievement didn't matter anymore. The most important focus was to follow through with my three main messages from my experience:

1-To love self and others unconditionally and non-judgmentally with the love I received on the other side;
2-To always seek knowledge; and
3-To live my life's purpose.

Given my new value system, it's no wonder when an old college friend called, I saw him in a different light. I was loving everything and everyone in the moment. When he asked me to marry him, I had no reason not to. It seemed like a short-term arrangement. I also reasoned, I needed a lot of care and had much healing to do. What a perfect opportunity to begin my life again with the support of a man who loved me.

I finished my college degree in communication and business and moved to Washington, D.C. with my new husband. I was learning that both my studies and my marriage were mismatched. Paul and I had many opportunities to experience our differences. His training was in engineering, which gave him an analytical, logical, left-brained approach to everything. His fun-loving approach to life allowed him to stay on the surface and never take anything or anyone too seriously. Emotion was a scary word for him; whereas I now had an extra sensitivity to everything and everyone. I found myself crying or emotionally moved by the smallest things. Movies like *The Sound of Music* or *The Wizard of Oz* brought me to tears.

I wanted to explain to him why my outlook on life was different from his; why I had trouble working in business and why I had been through ten jobs in a matter of five years. I knew I wanted to work with people in a meaningful way. Wherever I went, people opened up and told me their life's story. I was genuinely touched each time private information was shared. I wanted to make a difference, but I continued to move further away from the profound messages I received. I had these new-found insights, yet I wasn't able to put them into practice.

I certainly wasn't living my life's purpose. I didn't even know what that was. I wasn't getting more knowledgeable in anything. I was in a state of chronic pain with chronic health problems, feeling more frustration than love for myself. My energy and efforts were going everywhere but nowhere.

I knew an indescribable love, peace, joy and oneness for awhile. Yet as time went on, I was overwhelmed with rejection and grief for a place I longed to be.

I fell into a deep depression and withdrawal from life. I felt lost and rejected from the universe. I judged myself unmercifully. I wasn't good enough to remain in the heavenly sea of unconditional love and light. I was sent back. To what? To tennis? How shallow! Had I really felt fulfilled before this experience? Now all I felt was a big emptiness and void inside. How was I to share love, when I needed to physically heal and learn to love myself first?

What kind of knowledge was I to seek or know? What was my life's purpose? How was I to discover and fulfill my life's purpose? I had many unanswered questions and wanted them all answered. Why couldn't I remember all the universal knowledge and information I knew on the other side?

The next several years were filled with rehabilitation, physical therapy, diagnostic tests and reparative surgery. How could I plan for anything? The memories of the first operation always intensified with each successive surgery and I was about to undergo my fourth abdominal surgery. As a result of the original operation, the adhesions had stuck to my appendix and pulled it over to the left side of my abdomen. Also, on the left side, I had developed a grapefruit sized mass. With increased pain and decreased bowel function, I needed an immediate solution. My doctors recommended removal of the appendix and the mass. They wanted to rule out a cancerous growth. I knew deep inside that it wasn't a tumor. I wasn't afraid and strangely, I thought, I wouldn't be so lucky to die. After experiencing life beyond, I was far too eager for it.

I heard Wills' wisdom once again. "You can't take your own life... It's not your time yet... You have to go back and live your life's purpose." I knew I had to stay here and learn about life. I also knew death was a blessing for those who suffer. Yet, I needed to learn how to live life, not run from it.

After surgery, I was told the mass was a ball of adhesions. The adhesions had grown and stuck themselves into a mass, entangling my bowels. I was blessed. I didn't have a tumor. However, removal of the adhesions and appendix didn't solve the problem; it only gave temporary relief from the pain. I was told by the doctor that the adhesions could reattach to structures and create the same situation.

My recovery was slow because I was cut open from my navel to my pubic bone. I was no longer a candidate for laproscopic surgery. Laparoscopic surgery requires a blind entry. The doctor did not want to enter my abdominal cavity blindly, especially since my insides seemed to have a mind of their own, shifting and sticking at random. I wondered where the rest of my organs were, or would be, in the years to come.

Chapter 5

Lost in the Dark

I have been one acquainted with the night.
I have walked out in rain - and back in rain,
I have out walked the furthest city light.

-Robert Frost

After many hours of physical therapy, I contemplated my future. It was time to follow through with my messages. Was that the key to my health? I would start with message number one "to love others unconditionally... and share my message with others."

I wanted to share my experience of the light with my husband, Paul. I wanted to tell him how dear these messages were to me. I wasn't concerned that he was an atheist. I simply wanted to tell him what had happened. I gathered my courage and told him everything.

I was so anxious to come to terms with my past that I didn't anticipate a negative reaction from my beloved. It was worse than a negative reaction. He didn't believe anything I said. To make matters worse, he nicknamed me "psycho lady."

For three more years, until I turned thirty, I didn't talk to anyone else about my experience. I felt too vulnerable to expose myself again.

Paul and I moved back to Connecticut and lived with my parents. He joined my family's business and I decided to work on my second message, "To always seek knowledge."

I thought returning to school would fulfill that part of my mission and lead me into my life's purpose. I discovered that "seeking knowledge" was more than a college education with a degree. The meaning in the message was much deeper.

Time and again, I would experience this phenomenon I called "knowing" which goes beyond the five senses of consciousness. By accessing this universal knowledge through higher guidance and my own inner wisdom, my life would flow as easily as a stream after a springtime rain. Conversely, when I didn't pay attention to my inner knowing and listened to logic instead, I would end up fighting an upstream current. I would continue to fight this raging river for several more years.

I knew school would be difficult, especially since I was taking thirty-six prescription pills a day. Most days, I had difficulty staying in one position for any length of time. The forty-five minute commute and the hard plastic classroom chairs would be a challenge.

I was a chronic pain patient and western medical doctors labeled me an "incurable." They said, "There's nothing we can do about scar tissue, except operate and create more. Some people are more prone to it than others." And with an odd bent of humor, one of the doctors said, "You're lucky to be alive. You'll have to learn to live with the consequences. The only cure for you is to find the Holy Grail."

The consequences, of being more prone to it than others, had fairly large consequences. Dr. Naygee, an internist, told me, "When scar tissue restricts an intestine, a bowel obstruction can be created. Emergency surgery is required. The condition can turn into a life-threatening issue. You lose the ability for food to pass through and the obstructed bowel begins to die because of gangrene. Infection then has an opportunity to take over your entire body. This is called "sepsis."

I lived with a vicious, physical cycle. Every time more surgery was performed, more scar tissue was formed, creating a greater chance of restrictions in the future. The daily pain of abdominal pulling and intestinal twisting drove me forward in my search for healing. I wasn't terribly upset if my condition turned life-threatening. I wasn't afraid of death. Again, I heard my brother-in-law's wisdom, "It's not your time yet... You have to go back and live your life's purpose."

Before I could find my life's purpose, I had to follow through with the medical lawsuit I had filed after the original surgery. My family was supportive of my decision to follow through with litigation. However, I was torn between two issues. First, I didn't want to tarnish a doctor's reputation. Secondly, I didn't want Dr. Epsom to harm anyone else. I also felt financial compensation was due me. I couldn't get any medical insurance coverage because of the first surgery. I was $40,000 dollars in debt from the fourth abdominal surgery and owed my parents the twenty percent that their insurance company didn't pay from the first three surgeries.

The trial was in Hartford, Connecticut and lasted five days. I was tired and in pain. The valium kept me calm, the halcion helped me sleep at night and the pain killers dulled everything else. The first day of the trial, I was prepared to call the whole case off if Dr. Epsom apologized. After five years, I thought he might have had a revelation about his actions. His actions were more complicated than I had originally thought. Under oath, he admitted that he wasn't qualified to perform a laproscopy. He said he had changed my medical records and gave me pre-existing medical conditions on paper. He said, then the operation would appear to have a legitimate reason for execution.

No wonder medical insurance companies rejected my application! Not only did I have a chronic medical condition caused by the original surgery, I also had false documentation. I had never been in a hospital before this operation and now I couldn't stay away from them.

I learned more about my medical condition as the trial proceeded. Dr. Fummette, an expert and high-risk practitioner in obstetrics, rendered his opinion. He said, "A woman in her childbearing years, with the extensive, internal scarring that Laurelynn has, is at an increased risk for complications. If she were to get pregnant, there's a forty percent chance that she or the child would not survive."

I was shocked by those statistics. A deep grief welled up inside of me. I might not ever be able to have children! I know I didn't want to have children with my present husband but that wasn't the issue. I felt outraged that my choice may have been taken away. I looked over at Dr. Epsom with that new information. He had no expression on his face. I didn't understand how someone could be so devoid of emotion. The words "Go back and live your life's purpose," resonated in my head. I had assumed that parenting was part of my life's purpose but maybe parenting wasn't part of the big plan. I wasn't happy about that possibility. I needed a good cry before I could accept that my maternal drive and love for children may never be fulfilled.

The night before the trial ended, I had an offer from the defense to settle out of court for $250,000. My lawyer left the choice up to me. Although he strongly encouraged me to fight until the end, $250,000 was a great sum of money. I would be debt-free with additional money in the bank in case I needed any future medical care. I looked at my original intent. I wasn't after the money. If I accepted the offer, I would feel like I had sold my soul. I naively thought, "If I finish the trial and the doctor is found guilty, then he can't harm anyone else."

The next day, the judge ruled that Dr. Epsom was negligent, but he returned to his practice the following business day. I was awarded a paltry sum of money; and remained in debt.

After the lawsuit, I felt more lost than ever. I had no job, no career, no children, a marginal marriage, poor health and no home. I needed to put the past behind me and find a new direction in my life. I looked at the positive aspects. I had a supportive family and a loving memory of the light.

I returned to school at the University of Connecticut in Storrs. During one of my first trips to the college campus I found a health food co-op. I was guided to pick up a doctor's business card. Dr. Byron, a naturopathic doctor, worked with healing the body naturally through herbs, homeopathy and diet. I called him immediately. With Dr. Byron's guidance, I slowly weaned myself off all medication. After six months, I was living a very clean and natural lifestyle. I lost the thirty pounds I had gained post-surgically from all the medication.

I was more confident in my life's direction. I was accepted into a graduate program called Biophysical Science of Sport. I believed this major would rekindle my love for athletics. The program was theory-oriented, proving how the human body worked in various capacities. I was close, but this wasn't my life's calling. I liked the idea that I was studying about the human body but the classes seemed cold and technical.

One day, on the way to the human performance laboratory to do underwater body weighing, I noticed a sign on the bulletin board for physical therapy students. The sign listed all their internships at hospitals, nursing homes and sports clinics. Now this was something I'd like to do! I'd have direct experience with people. I knew I could make a difference. I also had an insider's view because I had been a physical therapy patient when I was going through my own rehabilitation. I never realized that by submersing myself in this new direction, I again was throwing myself further off balance.

Chapter 6

A Glimpse through the Window

Pure logical thinking cannot yield us
any knowledge of the empirical world;
all the knowledge of reality starts
from experience and ends in it.

-Einstein

The next five years, I dedicated to school and once again, ignored my body, my emotions and my spirit. I took out student loans, worked three part-time jobs and was a full time student at the University of Rhode Island in the graduate entry-level master's program for Physical Therapy.

Paul and I moved into a townhouse near the University. While I went to school and worked, Paul went to work and drank when he was home. Most of the time, I was too fatigued and in pain to notice, but with my athletic mind set, I was determined to follow through with three main messages from my experience. I desperately wanted to fulfill these messages so I could go home - home to the Light!

During the last year of school, I was confronted with many of my own healing issues. I pushed ahead regardless of what my body was saying, but I could no longer keep up the pace. I continuously learned from this pattern. I was torn between being happy about having a second opportunity in life and angry about my damaged body that required constant attention.

When a local Physical Therapist spoke to our class about craniosacral therapy and the mind-body connection, I knew I had to explore further. Martine Rini was involved in the local Rhode Island American Physical

Therapy Association. She was one of the first therapists to bring craniosacral therapy, myofascial release and somatoemotional release to the Rhode Island area.

I volunteered to be the demonstration for myofascial release. Martine, a kind and sensitive woman, exposed my abdomen so the twenty students gathered around could observe. The angry, red scar ran from the bottom of my sternum to the top of my pubic bone. Three years had passed since my last surgery. The half-inch wide scar was thick and raised and looked like it was only weeks old. As Martine manipulated the scar, I felt intense searing and burning pain.

Thoughts about the first operation drifted into my mind as, Martine told the class, "Sometimes when you work on an old injury, it's not unusual for the patient to re-experience the trauma or the memories."

I heard one of my classmates yell, "You better not work on her very long. Soon she'll be dead and float out of her body." Everyone chuckled.

I had confided in a few classmates that I had been clinically dead and watched the first surgery from the ceiling. I didn't expect everyone in this logical, scientific group to believe me. And as a result, gossip had spread rapidly.

With the jesting, I felt vulnerable. I didn't express any feelings about the treatment but I knew there was a truth behind what Martine had said. I was stunned by the power of the demonstration. I felt not only a physical change in the surface scar; I also felt an emotional shift.

I began seeing Martine or Marty as I came to know her, on a regular basis for "bodywork." I told her I was interested in personal growth and understanding on the mental, emotional, physical and spiritual levels. As the bodywork continued to uncover emotions, I felt the need to work with a psychotherapist. RoseAnna Semich, a motherly, feminine goddess type, exuded trust and gentleness. She had a broad understanding of metaphysics and had done her own astral traveling as a child. We were an instant match.

RoseAnna Semich and Martine Rini facilitated my inner personal work. I realized I'd held life's physical tension and emotional pain inside for a long time. I had been functioning in a dysfunctional way. Yet, just like in athletics, it was called survival. I was in denial about how my body felt. When I finally got in touch with my body, I realized how much pain I suffered every day. I shut off the pain to survive. Like shutting a window, I never realized how much I was stifling myself. When I experienced my first fresh cool gust of air, it took my breath away and burned my lungs. But the window was opening and the newness was welcoming. I was tired of suppressing what my body wanted to express. I didn't want to live like that anymore. I needed to find balance in my life. I needed healing on all levels. I wasn't prepared for what that would entail but I was committed. I wanted to go HOME.

During one of my first sessions with Marty, we moved beyond craniosacral work into an intense guided visualization and dialogue. I needed assistance with my healing so I called upon my "inner physician." I had no idea what or who an "inner physician" was but I went along with the idea. First I was guided to a comfortable, peaceful place. I let my imagination and my past experience take over. I was in the heavens with billowy clouds and a tranquil blue sky.

I heard Marty's voice in the distance, "Ask your inner physician to meet you."

Immediately, an old wise, white-haired man appeared on a cloud next to the one I was lounging on. He looked over a hundred years old with shaggy shoulder-length hair. But he was a spry fellow for his age. He had a youthful exuberance portrayed in his red spandex pants and blue tunic top. I was curious who he was. I heard Marty's voice again, "Ask him his name."

The first name that came into my mind was George. I asked, "George, who are you and what are you doing here?"

I am a higher, wiser aspect of yourself. Some might call me your "higher self," yet others might call me your "angelic self." Today, I've been labeled your "inner physician," and I'm here to help give you guidance with your own healing.

Does everyone have access to his or her higher self? I wondered. And how can I possibly do more for myself than what I'm doing?

George answered by taking me on a visual trip. We left the clouds and flew to earth. We went over tree tops, roof tops, and glided to a rocky cliff where we sat together, overlooking the ocean.

The ocean meets the heavens and the earth. Just as the universe is in perfect harmony so can your life be. Everyone has access to the higher aspect of themselves. Sometimes, however, people choose to ignore their natural, intuitive instinct and follow logic instead.

I chuckled, "I've been doing that for years." Then in a more somber tone, I said, "But I had a glimpse of another world once." I began to describe my light experience with a deep longing. I felt tears running down my cheeks. "All I've wanted to do since that time was to find my way back home," I sobbed.

My child, you are well loved. I am here to simply remind you. Home is not so far away.

I didn't understand, but his words were comforting. I felt an inner peace wrap me in an indescribable love.

Marty closed the session. I thanked her with a hug. She told me I had just experienced somatoemotional release. Somato whatever - I decided to learn all about these alternative therapies. One day I would give back and facilitate a powerful session for someone as Marty had done with me.

I felt as if I had stepped on an accelerated conveyor belt. I was rapidly learning about the mind-body-spirit connection, especially my own. I felt out of place at school. We were taught science and logic. I was going the other way, allowing my intuitive side to blossom. I again saw the rings of energy I once saw around people after my first operation. I tuned into the energetic dynamics among people. I didn't try to shut these strange phenomena down this time like I had when I was first married. I incorporated them into my life and allowed these feelings and this knowing to guide me, even in school.

One day, a classmate, Elayne Kinne, approached me. She said, "I know you were teased about floating out of your body, but my mother believes you had what is called a near-death experience." Elayne explained that her mother was part of a metaphysical community in North Carolina. The International Association of Near Death Studies (IANDS) was having a conference in a nearby town. She thought I might like to attend or seek out more information.

I couldn't go to North Carolina. I lived in Rhode Island. How would I justify a trip like that to my husband? To my surprise, an IANDS conference in Hartford, Connecticut was scheduled in the summer, a two hour drive from Rhode Island. I needed no justification for a short trip.

Also mentioned in the North Carolina brochure Elayne had given me was author, Dr. Raymond Moody and his book "Life after Life." I read his book a week later and was astounded by other people's similar experiences. I also discovered that one out of twenty American adults have had a near-death experience. And all this time, I thought I was alone.

I was excited but also apprehensive about the upcoming conference. I was afraid I'd be challenged. What if people there didn't believe me? What if they thought I had copied one of the stories out of Raymond Moody's book?

After evaluating my fears in a therapy session, I realized I would be in control. I was comforted knowing George would be with me, my now constant companion. Besides, I would go to listen; not speak. I would hang out, unnoticed in the back of the lecture halls.

Chapter 7

Seeing the Door

Nothing in life is to be feared,
only understood.

-Madame Marie Curie

I attended the Hartford, Connecticut IANDS conference in July of 1991. As I was driving my old, faded, yellow 1976 dented Chevy Nova, I reflected upon how my life had been nothing but a struggle since my near-death experience. I hoped I would get answers or clarity about the meaning of life - my life. I had told myself I was only going to listen but I knew I was going for more than that.

Things started heating up Saturday afternoon. Dr. Kenneth Ring, a researcher and founder of IANDS, brought a few of his research subjects to the conference. I sat in the back of the auditorium listening to the experiencers, as they were called. I saw a large, spherical golden ball of energy around the speaker's head. My sensitivity had increased because I was crying, listening to these touching stories. Yet my sensitivity reached beyond the five senses. I had seen this phenomenon before but never with such presence. My roommate for the weekend, Eileen Secor, told me I was seeing the woman's aura. Every time this woman talked about being with the light, her aura glowed brighter and pulsated bigger. It now stretched three feet above her head.

On our break, I leaned forward and glanced at the man and woman sitting in front of me. I noticed they had sketched the speaker and drawn a big circle above her head and labeled it aura. What a strange group of people. I had never said anything about seeing light around people, animals or plants, yet here it seemed to be a common phenomenon.

Many times during the weekend I was amazed on how much I had in common with these people. On a regular basis, I blew out light bulbs when I turned them on. I kept an extra supply in the closet. When I walked or drove under street lights, the bulbs would regularly black out. I never wore watches because they stopped working. I learned at the conference that these electro-magnetic changes were common for someone who had been to "the other side." All these strange quirks I had developed since my experience were not so strange after all. It was as if a rewiring had taken place.

Another effect I noticed was my increased sensitivity toward people. When I tuned into their spirit I could feel their emotions and their physical ailments. I also remembered most of my dreams and many times would receive personal messages or messages for others. I could also decide how my dreams would turn out (lucid dreaming). I learned that these were all common for near-death experiencers and also common for anyone who had a mystical or spiritual experience.

The highlight of the weekend was the support group for experiencers which met Saturday evening after the dinner banquet. I planned to attend but was not prepared for the shock in store. Eileen and I were late for dinner. We took the only two seats available. Introductions were made and I froze when the woman across from me introduced herself. She had the same last name as one of the doctors involved in my medical accident. I stared at her. I felt fear, anger and confusion as she asked me if anything was wrong. I replied a quick "No" and listened to the rest of the introductions.

A million thoughts raced through my head. Yet, at the same time, my thoughts couldn't move fast enough to clear the way. Could she be the wife of the doctor who set up this catastrophic accident? Her husband nearly kills patients and she comes to a near-death experiencers meeting! I didn't converse with anyone at dinner. I wasn't going to give anything away. To my surprise and relief, I overheard her say, "My husband still practices in Norwich and... I'm getting a divorce."

Only one doctor in town had that name. She was the innocent wife of that doctor! It wasn't her fault I had to physically suffer. Our chance meeting revealed one important point. I realized how much unresolved anger and confusion I had about this medical accident eight and a half years ago. I was visibly shaken but decided to attend the support group meeting.

I listened to everyone's story and felt a deep connecting oneness... something I hadn't felt for a long time. The support group was coming to a close but with a few minutes left I got a wave of inspiration and told the group "I'd like to speak, if anyone would care to listen."

For the next fifteen minutes, I told my story in a shaky, quavering voice. It was the first time I had spoken publicly. I was amazed to feel such a kind, loving atmosphere. The group gave me complete understanding and acceptance - a rare experience in the earth plane. Expressing my experience was emotionally difficult, but I knew I was going to be okay. After the session, many members of the group spoke to me, giving their encouragement, love and support.

The following is an excerpt from a letter that I sent to Bruce Greyson, M.D., coordinator of the conference:

I feel fortunate and grateful that I attended. I would like to thank everyone in the support group and all the speakers at the conference for brightening the path of enlightenment and reaffirming that healing is from within. I would like to share with you this dream I had Saturday night after speaking in the support group.

"I dreamed of a broken down, dilapidated red barn in the middle of a barren field. The barn had broken boards hanging loosely on its structure. The nails were rusty and loose. The field *was hardened and cracked with wisps of dried brown grass, growing sporadically from within the cracked clay. The grass desperately extended its lifeless blades upward. The sky was gray, stormy and threatening.*

As I viewed the barn from a distance, I saw a dull minuscule glow coming from within the barn, barely seeping out between the rotting boards. I walked toward the barn to investigate.

As I walked closer, the scene changed. The barn repaired itself. The dull red paint became vibrant. The old boards looked new and straightened. The barren field flourished into a meadow of long flowing green grass. Colorful wildflowers waved back and forth in the wind. Everything grew in harmony. The sky became a deep, rich peaceful blue. As I relished the spectacular scenery changes, a most extraordinary event took place. The glow in the barn transformed itself into a brilliant white light of beauty. Rays of light flooded the field and sky in perfect synchrony, steadily streaming outward from the barn, through every crack and seam."

It was a nice dream but I didn't know its meaning until Sunday's lecture. Nancy Evans Bush, President of IANDS, spoke. She said "It's time to clean house and we all have the power within us." At that moment, the dream flooded back to me, cleansing my spirit, giving me hope. The Barn represented me. I haven't opened the door yet or gone inside, but I'm on the right path. I'm getting closer, and the closer I get, the more healing takes place within. Again words don't seem adequate for the feelings of gratitude I would like to express, but will have to suffice for now- THANK YOU.

Before the conference ended, I was invited to attend the local support group at the University of Connecticut Health Center in Farmington under the guidance of Dr. Bruce Greyson. The group met the second Monday of every month. I felt like I had seen another glimpse of "HOME." All aspects of my life - the mental, emotional, physical and spiritual - would have to be confronted. I would begin with my marital relationship first.

Chapter 8

Restoration

It is only with the heart that one can see rightly. What is essential is invisible to the eye.

-Antoine de Saint-Exupery,
(*The Little Prince*)

After the conference, many events happened simultaneously. Again, I had tapped into my true essence. My life flowed like a magnificent work of art. Each new stroke increased my clarity and understanding. Thanks to my new brother-in-law, I meditated regularly twice a day. My sister, Gwen had remarried and her husband taught transcendental meditation.

When I meditated, I connected to the same kind of energy and peacefulness I had felt in my near-death experience. Meditation became the only stable influence in my life. Meditation not only guided me but also allowed otherwise difficult decisions to roll off my shoulders like raindrops rolling off a newly-waxed car.

Although my decisions came easily, the actions I needed to take were difficult. By the fall of 1991, my marriage had deteriorated beyond repair. Over several months, we discussed our differences every Sunday morning hoping to resolve them. We learned we had more differences than we had originally thought. I believed in life after death. Paul did not. I had priorities toward spirituality, self-growth, awareness and enlightenment. Paul did not. I was concerned about our environment; committed to a natural lifestyle; and wanted more than anything to be of service to the world. Paul told me, "Whatever is on this planet is for us. We don't need to be grateful to anyone or any universal power but ourselves." His lifestyle included beer, potato chips and fried bologna sandwiches. His new job, after being fired from my family's business, was working at developing gambling machines.

Maybe I was idealistic, but I knew my spirit needed to be aligned with my divine purpose. I'd rather live alone and have a harmonious lifestyle than curtail my life to anyone who did not align with the same core values. Participating in the near-death experiencers support group once a month gave me that alignment I needed and highlighted the disparity in my life I could no longer ignore. I met another man at the meeting, also named Paul, who was everything I longed my Paul to be. I knew my Paul was a kind person and had a good heart. Yet growing up with an alcoholic army father had hardened his views of reality. As our marriage counselor said, "Paul, you are in denial and may choose to be for the rest of your life."

I knew I couldn't change him. My marriage started because I accepted him non-judgementally and loved him unconditionally. I now understood the first part of my message, "to love myself unconditionally first." So for the love of myself and my spirit, I left my husband that December.

Also in December, I gave a lecture on the last day our class met. The lecture was called "The Near Death Experience and Health Care." I started the lecture by saying, "Nine years ago today, at exactly 11:00 a.m., I was clinically dead..." I was amazed at how the lecture impacted my classmates. Now that I had come to terms with my past, everyone else accepted it too. I'm sure it was no coincidence that the universe orchestrated the lecture to take place on the exact day and at the exact time nine years ago. Not by coincidence, I had a near-death experiencers support group meeting that night.

I went to the meeting early and met Paul from the group. We met alongside the Farmington River where he gave me a present. Inside the box, wrapped in pink floral tissue paper, was a small, delicate twig wreath decorated with red berries and miniature pine cones. He made the wreath from natural gatherings along the river. The postcard accompanying the gift said "As we flow to heaven's sea, share the light and love with me."

I was overwhelmed with emotion. How sweet for someone to know the importance of my NDE anniversary and to honor and share it intimately. Even though Paul was married, I experienced the meaning of love at a soul level. But my therapist had warned me that I was vulnerable. If I chose to pursue this new relationship, I was heading down a path of pain. And although I didn't pursue it, I still experienced pain for a love at a soul level that could not be consummated on a physical level. However, Paul and I remained good friends.

In retrospect, our meeting came at a crucial time. Although I couldn't be with this man, our short-lived relationship gave me a glimpse of what I knew my spirit and soul had always yearned for - love on a soul level.

I went to court in March of 1992 while in the midst of my internship. When the judge asked the grounds of my divorce, I answered, "We've grown apart physically, mentally, emotionally and spiritually." The judge chuckled. "That sums it up - divorce granted."

Paul didn't contest it. We split our debt and I gave him the dog. I wished him well with his life as he did with mine. We remained friends, something we always were but never grew beyond in the marriage.

I had time off before my last internship. I felt a need to be near the ocean - to purge and cleanse myself of my past relationships. I went to Florida where my parents spend the winters and received a nurturance of love that only mothers can give. The day after I returned home, I took the ferry to Block Island. It was a cold, windy Friday. With below freezing weather, snow on the ground and a stiff wind, the island was desolate. I walked from the ferry up to Mohegan Bluffs. I had forgotten bicycles weren't rented until Memorial Day, but with my long underwear, three pairs of pants and five jackets, I couldn't ride a bike. Two hours later, I arrived at the Bluffs and felt the salt-blown wind sting my face. I looked out over the rocky cliffs that plunged steeply into the ocean. The radiant sun, the cobalt sky and the crashing surf, had a mesmerizing and calming effect upon me. I looked up, arms outstretched and turned all my grief, turmoil and inner pain over to the sun, to the universe, to the higher power that I knew existed and said out loud "I'm in your hands. Please show me the way home - I surrender."

With those words, a gust of wind shot straight through my body. It whipped my hair against my windbreaker hood, making a loud flapping noise. I was thrown off balance. The universe answered me and the wind seemed to say -

"We hear you and understand your longing. Please trust in us - the universe."

As the wind dried the last of my tears, a figure walked up behind me. I wasn't frightened, just surprised to see another person outside in this cold, unwelcoming weather. He said, "Whatever you're going through, there's always a light at the end of the tunnel. I know, I'm a minister. I've counseled many people through their darkest hour."

I thought, I wouldn't call this my darkest hour. I was deriving great joy and benefit from my solitude with nature. Although, if he had seen me from a distance with my arms outstretched talking to the sun, he might have perceived the wrong idea. I wasn't going to jump but as I looked down, I was close to the edge. The wind must have shifted my position. I wanted to reassure this man he didn't have to perform a rescue mission. I told him, "I know the light. I've been to the other side. I'm just healing old wounds with nature's wisdom."

I don't think he was reassured because he was reluctant to leave. His parting words were, "God works in many mysterious ways. Keep the faith."

He spoke a truth, but I understood the meaning as "The **Universe** works in divine order, in ways we don't understand. **Trust.**" I left Block Island that evening with mixed feelings. I was excited about my journey ahead, and at the same time, felt a deep loneliness. I knew I was well guided - the universe sent a minister to the cliffs for support.

I also knew I was opening myself to a greater capacity to love myself and others. I was grateful I could stay at my parent's home while they spent the winter in Florida. I didn't want to live with them. I wanted a place of my own. I had to prove it to myself that I could make it without anyone's help.

It was difficult not to get depressed when all the questions crept in. Where would I live? Was I destined to spend the rest of my life alone? What type of work would I do? Could I physically take the demands of a full time job? How much money did I need to earn to survive? I put all these unanswered questions aside because, after graduation, I planned to travel in the southwest for the summer. I was going on an exploration, not only of the land, but an exploration of my soul's journey and life's purpose.

Chapter 9

Through the Doorway

Come forth into the light of things.
Let nature be your teacher.

- William Wordsworth

I was exhausted from the pressures of school, the emotional trials of a divorce and the action of turning my life upside-down. I had finished my last internship, and had graduated with a master's degree in Physical Therapy. I needed a rest. A cross-country camping trip with my friend Gail seemed like a good plan. I was in good company with Gail. We had much in common. We were recent divorcees, recent graduates and both on an undeniable spiritual journey. I had met Gail, a tall slender brunette with a gentle sensitivity, at my first internship. We became instant and lifelong friends. We were also unemployed and broke. We figured we had plenty of time to find jobs at the end of the summer. For now, we were without responsibilities to any place, job or person. The only responsibility we had was to ourselves, so we decided to enjoy our new found freedom and explore our country.

The first remarkable place we visited was Sedona, Arizona and its red rock formations. We had read about the energy vortices and the ancient dolphin energy and wanted to experience it. We set up camp in the middle of Sedona and for four nights we didn't sleep. We found Sedona's energy strong for our electromagnetically sensitive bodies. I got my period two weeks early and Gail vomited. Our dream state was also more vivid than normal. I repeatedly returned to this peaceful, jagged, rocky place. Filled with intense colors, the blending of blue, indigo and purple appeared in a circular, pulsating form outlined by a rocky border. Sometimes I sat at the bottom and looked up at these colors and felt the strength and security of the rocks. Other times I floated up into the depths of the colors and left the outline of the rocks behind and experienced freedom. During my meditations over the past year, I would visit this same place but now it was more intense, vivid and real.

The next day, we had an eight hour outing with a medicine man and he confirmed our concerns. "Always sleep outside Sedona," he said. "It's not only the energy vortices but all the 'spiritual seekers' (visitors) who bring their chaotic energy here to be dealt with as well."

One day, we stumbled across a cemetery. As I walked around the gravestones, I asked the universe to give me a sign about what to do next with my life. Many headstones had messages such as "Life is Short, Love is Eternal." They were all meaningful, but not until I rounded the last bend was a message revealed to me. A beam of light was coming from the headstone in front of me. As my attention was drawn to the light, I felt the sun's warmth reflecting on my heart. The name was "PERSONS" and the insignia was **"THY WILL BE DONE."**

I was moved with gentle force and assurance. I froze in my tracks, took a gasping mouthful of air, got goose bumps all over and felt tears well up in my eyes and spill down my cheeks. This was the same message I received in my daily meditations. The message didn't tell me exactly what to do next but it was a confirmation. I would continue to listen to the universal messages and follow the divine plan - whatever that was and wherever that would take me. At that moment, I understood, as if the magnetic red rocks of Sedona, towering among the cemetery, were saying:

Life is not only an individual pursuit but a surrendering to a power higher than yourself. Sometimes during your most challenging moments, after you quit fighting and

controlling the outcome, your greatest insight and under-
standing comes.

I thanked "Persons," and felt grateful for the universe's continued guidance.

Fatigue was a daily reminder of how desperately my body needed rest and healing. I kept pushing to fulfill my life's purpose which took on a whole new light, "Thy will be done." Whatever I was supposed to do, I would, but only if guidance came directly from the universe. I was still in a quandary though, because I needed to discern what was guidance and what was not.

After Sedona we drove to the Grand Canyon. We slept in our van, in the parking lot, next to the Canyon's edge. We wanted to view the Canyon in the early morning before the droves of people arrived. Since grade school, I had read about the Grand Canyon but no picture book or written words were adequate preparation for the magnificent vastness it portrayed. The place had an unbreakable stillness and tranquility. No sound of vehicles or airplanes or humanity was heard. Every so often, a chirping bird would peep to confirm the silence. The Grand Canyon reminded me of an early morning on Mooselookmeguntic Lake where I spent my summers with my grandparents. I would revel in the stillness of the lake, smooth as sculptured ice with the morning mist slowly lifting. The only sound was a distant loon calling for its mate. Both places had the same mystical, peaceful quality.

As fast as I settled into the serenity, the stillness ended. The earlier chirping sounds turned into ear piercing cawing. A group of seven ravens descended on a neighboring rock. I wanted to soak up the last minutes of solitude because I knew shortly we'd have to deal with bus loads of tourists. The precious time of quietness and reflection was like aloe vera gel, absorbed by a sunbaked body. I thirsted for more, but these birds weren't going to allow it.

What were they doing here? There weren't any dead carcasses or trash around. Gail and I decided to continue our walk around the canyon's edge. As soon as we moved, the big black ravens squawked in unison, left their rock, and flew beside us, ahead of us and behind us. When we stopped, they stopped. When we walked, they flew and cawed to us. Our annoyance turned into laughter and then wonder. We looked at each other and a knowing dawned on our face.

"Remember what Dawson (the medicine man) told us yesterday," Gail said.

"Refresh my memory," I said. And a smile crossed my face.

Gail imitated our shamanic prophet. "He said, 'Pay attention to the animals, the birds and the creatures - for they will bring you many messages on the remainder of your journey.'"

"But what's their message?" Gail asked

I stopped walking, put my foot up on a nearby rock, rested my elbow on my leg and propped my head up on my fist. I was poised for deep thought but nothing came. I finally said, "I don't know. I guess the ravens have to tell us or at least show us something."

We put the universe to the test and decided these magical birds would take us to our next destination. We followed nine successive ravens. Where they flew, we drove. They lead us to Winslow, Arizona and "The Meteorite Crater." The six mile approach to the crater took us through barren fields of flat plains grass. Upon closer inspection, a few lonely, stray cows were nibbling away at clumps of once green grass. The sky was misty gray with beams of light shining through, beckoning us to come closer. Electrical activity was all around, but not at the crater, "my crater" I would soon learn. The light, once again, lead the way for our guidance. As I parked the car and stepped out of the vehicle, I got a warm tingling all over as if to confirm "Yes - something magical was about to happen."

We paid our four dollars to observe the 49,500 year old crater. We went to the observation deck and to our dismay learned the crater floor was closed. However, we could take the three and a half mile perimeter walk. We walked the crater alone and at our own pace. I was awed at the sight. This was the place I had dreamed about two days earlier and the same peaceful place I had been frequenting in my meditations for the past year. I wasn't dreaming. My eyes were open. I patted the nearest rock several times to make sure I was awake. How strange. I knew every jagged edge, rock pile and bumpy terrain of this crater. I climbed on top of the white boulder that my spiritual guide George had sat on many times before in my meditations. He represented a higher, wiser aspect of myself. I felt his strong spiritual presence. I sat with the wind blowing my hair out of my eyes. I sobbed a gentle cry of thankfulness to all my guides, higher power, God and the universe for leading me to "my crater." It was always a time of peaceful remembrance and significant input when I found myself visually resting in this place.

The peaceful remembrance allowed reflection upon a place and time of all-knowing, all love and all oneness. Yet I was glimpsing and understanding this place was not so far away. Maybe by searching and seeking, I was missing something in front of me.

Significant input came from nature during my crater walk. The sun peeked out from behind the bleached billowy clouds and the shadows formed the shape of a butterfly on the crater floor representing transformation to me and for me. The next two hours were an inner transformation, a death and a rebirth of my spirit. It was also the beginning of my consciously conversing with nature and spirit guides.

"Okay, what do I need to do today at my crater?" The word **Release** came as the northeast wind howled in my face. I was amazed how the wind changed directions so quickly and the answers came so clearly. I needed to release all the old scars from my relationship and past medical history.

I sat on the rock, looking at the crater. The three-hundred sixty degree view had unique vegetation. The northwest rim was plush with green grass, trees, and evergreen bushes. The southwest rim was desert-like with white and tan rocky clay. My attention was drawn back to the southwest corner where I noticed beams of white light solely illuminating an ordinary evergreen bush. It was more than an aura. The life force of this single bush in a place devoid of much vegetation emanated an intense energy. The vibrancy of pulsing light was radiating outward. I was reminded of the "burning bush" that Moses encountered on Mount Horeb. Would there be another message? When I reached the bush, the glow pulsed stronger. I saw one rock the size of a plum under the bush. The oblong rock was perfectly divided in half with a strange chalkwhite color on top and a grayish brown color on the bottom. A straight line was etched around its circumference. I bent down and reverently picked up the rock. I cradled its warmth in the palm of my hand. I heard the words in my head, felt the words from the rock and knew the words from the "burning bush" -

Always keep the lightness above the darkness. Always choose love over fear.

As I finished my walk, deep in thought, I barely noticed the raven gracefully flying beside me. I jumped from the sound of a loudspeaker, but didn't see anyone. I reflected back on the words spoken in a gentle, strong, caring and all-knowing manner-

BE PATIENT MY CHILD.

The voice was familiar and the message was clear- "Be patient. Everything is unfolding. You are on the right path."

I didn't think to ask who was sending this message. One year later, I learned this presence was the same presence that greeted and surrounded me in my near-death experience. It wasn't my brother-in-law, Wills. This presence was a guardian of many spirits in the physical and spiritual realms. I would come to know this spirit as Methuselah, an ascended master and steward of our spirit family.

After my crater walk I thought I would receive information from Methuselah regularly. "Patience" was the correct word of encouragement. I had more health trials in store before I would be able to accept and receive divine guidance.

Chapter 10

Inside

The womb is the first home.
Thereafter, home is the soil you come from and recognize,
what you knew before uprooted...
Each home is an unrepeatable configuration;
it has personality, its own emanation,
its spirit of place.

- Lance Morrow

We continued our trip to Canyon De Chelly, the Four Corners (where New Mexico, Arizona, Utah and Colorado meet), Mesa Verde and Arches National Park in Utah. We were setting up and tearing down camp every day or two and were fatigued beyond words. We took out our map of the Southwest, closed our eyes and let our finger point to the next spot. We needed a place to rest and rejuvenate for at least a week.

We pointed to Pinedale, Wyoming, seventy miles Southeast of Jackson Hole, Wyoming. We had no idea what was there, but as was typical we trusted that the universe would take care of us. I felt transported to heaven when we drove through the hills of Wyoming. There were no houses, just miles of prairie grass covering rolling hills. The music *Heart of Perfect Wisdom* by On Wings of Song and Robert Gass was playing on the van's cassette player. The harmony of the choir brought us higher until we reached rugged mountains, the last traces of snow on the ground. We kept driving, trusting that rest was in store.

We found a ranch called Elk Ridge Lodge, bordering on the Green National Forest and the Continental Divide. We arrived prior to their busy season, so they only charged us forty dollars a night. The private log cabin, home-cooked meals and leisurely walks in the woods were just what we needed before traveling to Denver, Colorado. I had a professional engagement at the American Physical Therapy Association's National Conference to present research I had done while in school. I wasn't happy about my obligation.

What a shock returning to "civilization!" All the realities which we had managed to escape for a month, flooded back to us in Denver. We were plagued with questions about our future - not only from ourselves but from our colleagues. Where were we going to live? What type of job would we get? How much money did we need to make? When did payment on our student loans come due?

I had no answers for any of those questions, but the answers came in my dreams. I dreamed of my last internship and the woman that owned the private practice. While in school, I had attended many outside workshops to learn alternative healing therapies. When I dreamed of doing hands-on-healing, cushioned in the Physical Therapy term "manual therapy," I knew I would pursue this path further.

My hesitation in my awake state was that the woman had a strong personality. Although she was kind and loving, I could see conflict as an employer-employee relationship was established. I was also concerned because her practice was in the same town where my medical accident took place. I would have to face many of my ghosts from the past including the doctors. I reasoned that taking the job was something I needed to do to be free of the past.

After three dreams in a row, I was reassured the job would work out. I called my future employer from Denver and set up a meeting with her upon my return. For now, I would work with my hands in a clinic for people who had chronic pain and illness.

Now that one burden was out of the way, I decided to enjoy the rest of our journey in the southwest. Gail and I were thankful to leave the city. On our way out of Denver, we drove past "Journey Bookstore" and decided the name fit our lifestyle so we stopped.

As we walked around the store, I heard the click of a new cassette tape broadcasting over the store's speakers. The first song played with such sweet innocence. A knowing reached the depths of my heart. The music stirred a recognition and feeling of oneness.

I went to the store attendant and said in the middle of the first song, "Sir, I'd like to buy that tape."

He said, "I'm sorry, Miss. It's not for sale. It's a demo we received in the mail yesterday. This is the first time I've played it."

"Oh," I said disappointed. "Please, I just have to have it. It's so beautiful." I gave him my warmest smile.

"Well, I suppose we can get another demo...but I'll have to charge you five dollars."

"That's great," I said enthusiastically with appreciation.

"Don't you want to listen to the rest of it to be sure you want it?"

"Oh no," I said. "I'm sure!"

He smiled with understanding "Would you like anything else?"

"Yes, this book *Emmanuel* by Pat Rodegast."

"That's a good choice," my new friend said with encouragement.

I thanked him and we were on our way. As soon as we were driving, I played the new tape. The music moved me to tears within minutes. The chorus is as follows:

The oceans are calling,
with millions of voices.
The oceans are calling,
it's time to go home.

Dare to dive in,
through the fear and the darkness,
for diving within,
you will find your way home.

Someone else understood. Someone else wanted to go home. Yet there was a new recognition. Although it sounded like home was a place in the ocean, metaphorically I understood it as, "We are living in the sea of darkness and in order to go home we need to dive inside. Find the light within ourselves."

I wanted to find out more about this person who knew about "Going Home." I read the title of the tape. It was called *Delphys- Ocean Born*, The Songs of Cathie Malach and Kim Rosen with Amy Fradon and Leslie Ritter, Vocalists. The dedication on the inside cover thanked Emmanuel and Pat. How strange? I just bought a book called *Emmanuel* by Pat. I later learned that it was the same Emmanuel and Pat. Kim Rosen does self-growth workshops around the country with them.

We continued to drive for miles, noticing the changing landscape from dry, arid desert to rich green, pine trees. We were headed for the Black Hills of South Dakota. Mount Rushmore was advertised for many miles before we arrived so we decided to take a "peek." There was a sadness to viewing the man-made decimated mountain carving of presidential men. Looking at man's creation was amazing; yet the contrast of looking at the natural beauty of unspoiled land and forest gave me another feeling. A feeling of peace, tranquility and respect, something our world needed desperately, was portrayed in the surrounding mountains.

We set up camp that night with a strange feeling of betrayal. Our white ancestors took the Native American land and have since destroyed, not only the race, but all of the surrounding nature. In the camp lodge, we saw a picture of a cowboy next to a pile of buffalo carcasses stacked as tall as a three story building. The cowboy was smiling proudly of the work he had done.

I felt an anger and almost a responsibility for someone else's deeds. Then the following words came to me.

What is done is done. You have lived many lives and know the feelings on each side. What is important now is to move forward with peace and harmony. You are as much Native American as your brothers and sisters born beside you. You can only make a difference by understanding yourself. When you understand, respect and love yourself you will understand, respect and love all people and all of nature.

That evening, a hail storm, mixed with sleet and snow, pounded our tent. We moved into the van and stored our clothes in the tent. The storm turned into a torrential downpour with thunder and lightening echoing in our green, metal cargo van. It was as if all the ancestors' torment and my pain I had carried for others' actions were being stripped away with each thunder clap. The storm finally turned to a gentle rain, bringing us cleansing and release.

My release didn't come easily. I suddenly experienced a ferocious pulling pain in my lower right abdomen. The pain was familiar and intense. The adhesions in my belly were pulling and restricting my intestines. They were sticking to my muscular wall of my abdomen, and every time I breathed,

I received a painful reminder of my plight. I wasn't sure why it was acting up now. All I wanted to do was release the pain. I knew I had been pushing my body on this trip. I was in an old pattern. Was my body telling me to slow down and listen to its needs? I had a chronic vaginal yeast infection since the start of the trip so that was my first indicator that I was out of balance.

Gail was unsure what to do. She lovingly supported me and said, "Let me know if I need to take you to an emergency room."

I said with a strained smile, "I will, thank you." I was fortunate to have such an understanding, caring friend. Gail had done her own processing on the trip, and we had developed healthy boundaries with each other. We knew when to push and when to listen.

The pain didn't let up, so I said out loud to the universe, "I am willing to do whatever I'm supposed to. Please let this pain go away and I promise my body, I will slow down."

By the morning, the storm had passed and so had my pain. I was feeling miraculously recovered. Gail suggested we have an easy day. I said, "Oh, I'm much better. Let's go hiking."

"But I thought -" Gail started to say.

"I know Gailie, I'm really feeling better."

Against my body's inner knowing and ignoring Gail's better judgment, we preceded to hike the 8,000 foot Harney Peak. The misty, magical path wound through gigantic, vibrant pine trees. Halfway up the mountain, I left the trail to relieve my full bladder. As I stood up, sparkles of sunlight, at the base of an uprooted tree beckoned me forward. I shouted to Gail. Over fifteen large clusters of rose quartz crystals were hanging from the rooted soil. I felt like we had found that elusive pot of gold at the end of the rainbow. The rocks communicated this message:

Our purpose in revealing ourselves to you is to remind you about love. We are full of love. You are near empty and need to rebuild your internal resources. To bring healing, love yourself first. Then, like us, you can give love to others. Take a few pieces with you to always remember.

Eight hours later, we finished the hike, exhilarated and exhausted. We still had to go back to camp and deal with our wet clothes. We had stayed dry in the van the night before but our clothes hadn't fared so well in the tent. We strung ten lengths of rope across the center of our cargo van and air-dried our now musty smelling clothes as we drove.

The rest of our trip was a blur. I no longer had the energy to sightsee. We drove to Montana and we were less than a hundred miles from Yellowstone National Park. But we were too fatigued to visit. I wanted to go home - wherever that was - and rest.

Chapter 11

Internal Renewal

If the doors of perception were cleansed,
everything would be seen as it is, infinite.

- William Blake

Gail and I flew back from California to Connecticut. I was in need of healing. I had constant pain in my abdomen from the scar tissue. I was also in a state of chronic fatigue and suspected a chronic yeast infection. Ignoring all my symptoms, I went to northwestern Maine for my family's traditional Fourth of July gathering. I needed rest before I settled into a work routine.

My body continued to scream for attention. I wondered if I could have a sexually transmitted disease (STD) since I did have relations with David, a waiter I had met during my last internship.

A master's degree in the health care profession, and an AIDS seminar didn't prevent me from failing to use protection. I was surprised at how far I had drifted away from logic. The only solace I had was trusting my guidance. I checked in with the universal knowledge and knew it was safe to have sex with this man, so I did.

As a teenager or young adult, I had never experimented with sex. I was too involved with sports. David was the only other man I had been with besides my exhusband. He was new and exciting. I realized in that moment, how difficult it must be for teens, single people or the gay community to be confronted with life and death choices from a single act of romance.

A few weeks later, my knowing was confirmed. My gynecologist told me I didn't have the HIV virus or any sexually transmitted disease. I realized having "knowing" or not, it was far better for me to practice safe sex.

While in Maine, in the haven of my grandparents cottage, I volunteered to stay up one night and tend to the fire. Sitting in the green and brown cloth bean bag chair beside the fireplace, feeling the last hints of warmth from the fading embers, I wrote in my journal. After finishing my last entry, I turned the page and with my eyes closed, had my pen poised with my non-writing hand on a blank page. As I silently asked for guidance and strength for the upcoming months, my pen moved. I opened my eyes to see unfamiliar but legible handwriting on the paper:

We are here to give you love. To give all the love in the universe channeled through your hands. We will let you know when everyone is listening. You will know. Listen also. Yes, we'll come again.

I went to sleep that chilly July night with a warmth of reassurance. Whatever I had to face in the upcoming months, I would be well-supported and guided.

I returned to Connecticut and met with my future employer. We agreed I would start working full time at the end of August. Until then, I would use the next five weeks to continue my own healing and find a place to live. After many years of stress and tension in a disharmonious household, I looked forward to creating a sacred space for myself.

I was still seeing RoseAnna, my psychotherapist and began seeing Carol Allwell, an acupuncturist in Newport, Rhode Island for my healing. RoseAnna suggested I begin with "one step at a time" to find my living quarters. Like in Wyoming, I decided to let the universe guide me.

First I took out a local map and circled Norwich, the town in which I would work. I used my rose quartz crystal pendant and dowsed the map, something I had learned from an old Indian on my trip west. It pointed to

Voluntown, Connecticut, a small country farm town about twenty miles northeast of Norwich. When I drove out to Voluntown, past all the fields of corn bordered by stonewalls, I felt a deep peace. And when I drove past the petite, white steepled church in need of paint and repair, yet standing tall and proud on a hill dated 1775, I felt a kinship.

I grew up in Canterbury, a neighboring town, so I knew Voluntown had a lake, although the lake was called Beach Pond. I always had an affinity to water, so I drove around the lake first. I drove by houses and cottages sitting on the lake's edge. I continued down the hill. The lake was on my right. I stopped, rolled down the windows and looked out at the glistening blue lake with its pine forested islands. I took a deep breath, smelled the faint pine scent and listened to the gentle breeze. I closed my eyes. This felt so right.

As I pulled away on the half-dirt, half-tarred road and looked behind me, I noticed a small brown house with a deck overlooking the lake. I froze. I had seen that house before in my dreams. I had that dream when I was married and never quite understood it. I was living in that house alone, peacefully, beside a lake. Why would I be happily living in a house by myself? I never forgot the dream because there was an inner peace, a feeling of "home" that was everlasting.

I sighed. "I wish you were for rent." Obviously someone was living there, for the grass was mowed and a fresh coat of white trim had recently been applied.

I drove back to my parents' house, elated I had found the right area but disappointed I couldn't live in my "dream" house. I would look in the paper tomorrow, maybe I'd find a house or apartment on the same street.

As soon as Chucky's local convenience store opened at six in the morning, I bought a paper. I immediately looked for rentals under Voluntown. Three were listed. The first rental was in an apartment house and the second rental was a duplex. But the third rental caught my eye. "One bedroom house for rent. Call for showing," read the ad.

As soon as nine o'clock rolled around, I called. "Yes, I have a one bedroom house for rent," said the man. "We just had it fully renovated. It used to be my father's house. He passed away two months ago."

"When can I look at it?" I asked excitedly.

"Let's see...today happens to be my day off. Can you meet me at about three o'clock after I pick up my son."

"Sure," I said. "See you then."

At two o'clock, I headed toward Voluntown in my faithful Nova. I only needed twenty minutes to get to Voluntown from Sterling but I wanted to leave plenty of time. I didn't remember the names of the roads I had been on yesterday so I wasn't sure of the directions. But, I knew it had to be in the same vicinity.

As my clunky car rattled along, I suddenly thought about my appearance. What kind of impression would I give the landlord, if I drove in an old junk car and told him I was unemployed? I never asked him the rental price. Maybe I should have taken my parents' car for the afternoon.

No, I knew I needed to do this on my own. Besides, making a false impression was never my style. I always believed if someone couldn't know you for who you were, regardless of appearances, then the relationship was best to be avoided.

I was looking for telephone pole #73, but lost count of the numbers coming down the hill. I saw a tall man with a mustache and a toddler on the front lawn of my "dream" house. The man was putting a ladder away and the toddler was happily following him. "A nice family lived there," I thought.

I stopped the car, rolled down the window and yelled to the man. "Do you know where pole #73 is on Bennett Road? I'm supposed to meet someone and look at a house for rent."

He pointed to a pole on his left, as the wind parted a vine from covering the number 73. He smiled and said, "I've been meaning to cut that vine. Prospective renters have a hard time finding this place."

I said in disbelief, "This is the place?"

He nodded.

"This is great!" I said, without any reservation.

I parked the car and got out. "Hi, I'm Laurel. You must be Craig."

"Yes. Do you know this place?" Craig asked out of curiosity.

"Kind of," I hesitated. "I grew up in this area."

"It's the first time we've had the house for rent. My Dad broke his hip and while he was recovering, we refurbished the place. A week before he moved back in, he died from a massive heart attack."

"Oh - I'm sorry but I'm sure he's in a good place," I said.

"He was eighty-six years old and was failing the past year."

"He must have been a kind man yet loved his solitude," I said without thinking.

"Yes, that describes him quite well. Going to a nursing home was difficult for him while his hip healed. He hated to give up his independence."

Then as if we had been friends for a lifetime, I blurted out, "I feel his presence. He's at peace now."

He looked at me with eyes that filled with tears. "Yes, I think he is too. Thank you. Anyway, let's go inside. I'll show you around."

The place had a charming character. Forty-six stone steps zig-zagged up a slope and lead to a side door. The back door exited at ground level into a private backyard with the potential for a vegetable garden. The house was bordered by a once well-kept perennial garden. Once inside, I was immediately drawn to the sliding glass doors, that opened up onto a deck. A magnificent panoramic scene unfolded. I turned my attention back to the inside of the house. The layout was simple but perfect. The kitchen, bathroom and bedroom had been remodeled which gave the place a freshness. Craig's wife had hung curtains.

After the tour, Craig said, "Would you like to rent the place? You'd be the first renter. I'd like you to live here. Someone else was interested but their references didn't check out."

I said, "Do you need references?"

"No, references aren't necessary. Sometimes when you meet someone you just know," Craig said.

"How much is the rent?" Craig glanced at my car, "We were asking $525/month but if $475 is easier, we can do that."

"Perfect. Thank you so much. Is there anything else? Do you want to know about my job?"

"Only if you want to tell me."

Craig and I continued our conversation, sharing our life's philosophy.

I moved in the next week. My older brother, Gig, gave me furniture and helped me set up house. I was glad my family lived nearby, but I was also glad to live by myself. After thirty years, living alone was a prescription I yearned to fill.

I wondered if I'd be frightened or lonely. Craig had told me the lake is pretty desolate after labor day. A single woman, living alone, on a back country road without street lights seemed like a foolish proposition to some. But I wasn't afraid. I had been guided to live here. Whatever the universe had in store for me, I would handle.

One month after I began work, I decided to remedy loneliness. I called Craig. "Hello, I've decided to take your suggestion and get a pet. It would be nice to have company during the fall and winter months."

"That's fine. A cat would work out well. I'm afraid a dog would be too messy in the house," Craig said apologetically.

"Oh, I don't want either of those. I'd like to get a Vietnamese potbellied pet pig." I held my breath.

"Did you say pig?"

"Yes," I said excitedly and rambled off all the details about how clean, smart and how they are easily litter box trained.

He said, "Wait, wait...slow down. That's fine. I've read about those pigs and know what you're saying."

"Oh, thanks," I said with relief.

"Do you think my kids can come see it?"

"Sure, I'd love to show them the pig. I was planning to pick her up this weekend if you gave me the okay."

In late September for my birthday present, I picked up "Winnie-the-Pig." She was a one and a half pound shy, lovable piglet. She was black with white markings above each hoof and had a white dot in the middle of her forehead. Her middle name became "ajna" which meant third-eye in sanskrit.

I felt fulfilled in my home life. Work was a different story. The first day I started my job, I inquired about Dr. Epsom. "Does Dr. Epsom still work in Norwich? And does he refer patients to our clinic?" I asked.

"Did you read today's paper?" a colleague asked me.

"No, why?"

"He died yesterday from a long term illness," she answered.

Funny, I was ready to confront my past and Dr. Epsom died the day before I got into town. All I wanted to do was thank and forgive him. My life was better and although I still had health problems, I didn't blame him anymore. I realized how valuable my health trials and struggles had been. I was awakening to a greater awareness. Dr. Epsom just happened to be a player. As RoseAnna my therapist suggested, I wrote him a letter in my mind, communicated it to him on the spirit level and had closure with him.

RoseAnna sensed my increasing fatigue and pain and questioned me about my work schedule. I was treating ten to twelve people a day. And although I knew about not taking on other people's "stuff," I continued to get weaker and weaker. My clients were feeling better. I was feeling worse. I loved my work, but I had to work too many hours to meet my financial obligations. I had created more stress in my life by being on my own. The more I worked, the more exhausted I became. With less energy, I tapped into more pain.

I spiraled down to a chronic pain state again. Carol, my acupuncturist, emotionally supported me. She said, "I understand how difficult it is for you. If you choose not to be here on this earth plane, I support you."

RoseAnna, was supportive also but took a different approach. She asked me, "What keeps you here?"

I didn't have an immediate answer. I was grieving for home, for the light - where there wasn't any pain, only love and freedom. I had my family, thank God. But I knew I needed to find a reason within myself that would keep me here. For a couple of weeks, I wasn't sure if I wanted to remain living in my physical form. I appreciated nature and felt life was a gift when one was in good health. But when one was in pain, it was difficult to see beyond the pain. I heard Wills' voice once more, "You can't take your own life. You have to go back and live your life's purpose."

And then as I sat in my living room, I looked at Winnie. Like many animals, she seemed to know when I was having a bad day or was exhausted from work. She jumped up onto my lap and snuggled to one side or another, wherever I hurt. Her warmth, energy and unconditional love penetrated my being, renewing hope and faith. She was an immediate reason to stick around. She was a gift.

Another unexpected gift came to me in the midst of my pain. One Saturday morning, in late October, during my morning meditation, I heard the words, "Write to the personal ad in the paper. Write to the ad." I knew what advertisement that phrase implied...

Four weeks ago, I went to my mailbox. This particular afternoon, I got out of work early and was joyfully anticipating receiving correspondence. Living alone made me look forward to reading my mail. I decided I would sit on my deck, sip herbal iced tea, feel the last bit of warmth from the lingering sun and leisurely go through my mail.

I opened my bright blue mailbox with orange letters my brother had found at an auction for me. To my disappointment, there was no personal mail only a local newsprint circular. The paper, called "AT HOME," had an ironic ring and added to my growing irritation. Reluctantly, I took out the paper and folded it in half for the trash. As I climbed up my steps, I decided not to let the mail ruin my afternoon. Maybe the universe wanted me to read the paper.

Local news and home town stories were portrayed. Nothing special caught my eye until the last page labeled "The Singles Connection." I chuckled out loud and Winnie grunted in reply. This was good entertainment after all. I read through the ads with a lightness of heart, wishing all the seekers success. In the middle of the column was an ad that was different from the rest. This man wasn't interested in "romantic walks on the beach" or "dining out over candlelight."

His script was simple and straightforward and read as follows:

Code 34279 - Divorced white male, 39, 5'10", long brown hair, hazel eyes, non-smoker, non-drinker, somewhat shy. Interested in healthy natural living, vegetable gardening, jazz, blues, harmonica. Looking for slim, caring, sincere, attractive white female with similar interests, 30-45 for lasting relationship. Photo with letter would be appreciated.

I wondered, "What type of man was behind the words? How long had his ad been running? Had anyone answered him? And had he found his mate?"

I also wondered what he looked like. There was something romantic about a man with long hair. I had always pictured myself with a longhaired earthy type - a long way from an exhusband who wore an army crew cut.

I stopped all my thoughts. "Get real," I told myself. "I know the universe works in mysterious ways but a personal ad?" I had never answered one before and had only heard about all the trouble and sometimes frightening experiences one could encounter.

I got up from my deck chair and walked straight into the kitchen. Winnie came running behind, grunting with delight. I opened the cabinet door under the sink and threw away the paper. Living alone was turning me into a desperate woman, I thought. I didn't need anyone. I was convinced if the universe intended for me to have a relationship - it would just drop into my lap. For now Winnie and I were doing fine. I went back to the deck with my journal and wrote about everything but that distracting local paper.

Over the next few weeks, I found myself thinking about that ad and the man behind it. I didn't even know him or probably ever would, I told myself. But my attention drifted back to the gentle, sensitive energy that exuded from the words that I had read on that quiet fall afternoon. Every week, I found myself secretly looking forward to receiving "AT HOME." Once considered junk mail, I now saved the paper. I immediately checked the personal ad section to see if his script was still running. Funny how that paper took on top priority over all my other mail. The fourth week and all was well. His ad was still in print. In a strange way, I was comforted...

"Write to the personal ad. Write to the ad in the paper," I heard the words again and was drawn back to the present. Reluctantly but also excitedly, I followed my inner guidance and wrote a letter to #34279. I decided since I was going beyond logic, I would be as truthful and as straightforward as words would allow. The letter read like this...

Hello. As I sit on the floor, after my morning meditation, staring out the sliding glass doors, viewing the lake with serenity and peace - I wonder why I feel compelled to write this letter.

I'm quite content in my rented, one bedroom house in the country with Winnie Ajna, my Vietnamese pot-bellied pet pig. I've been alone for almost a year now but as I look back on my marriage I realize my aloneness started long before the marriage was over.

I have no bitterness or anger over that relationship - instead just a gratefulness for the opportunity to learn and grow. It's been a healthy experience for me to be alone and come to a better understanding of who I am. I, however, miss a friendship, a confidante, someone to share the beauty of nature with, to talk about life's meaning and purpose.

Winnie is a good listener, but I don't know if she appreciates a moonlit night on the lake or an early morning sunrise with the birds chirping outside my bedroom window. She's a very special animal friend and gives that unconditional love that seems so difficult to find in human relationships.

As far as spirituality goes, I've had some eye opening events in my life. The most significant has been my near-death experience ten years ago. After experiencing an out of body existence, traveling to a different dimension and being with the most brilliant beautiful golden light of unconditional love and peace, it had a way of changing my life.

I think all religions are okay. Whatever works for that person. I think ultimately we're all here to learn from each other, to grow and to honor the light by approaching everyone and everything with love.

I don't belong to a formal religion and instead find my church is within and my spirituality lies deep at the core of my existence and seems to be enhanced when I'm with nature.

I took a two month trip out west this summer and tried to absorb all of God's universe. It was spectacular - from the hikes in Yosemite to the horseback riding in the hills of Wyoming. I think it's so important for us to take care of Mother Earth and live simply. A book I once read *Voluntary Simplicity - Outwardly Simple, Inwardly Rich,* portrays a deep caring for our world.

It's difficult to know more about you with a few lines in a newspaper as it probably is difficult to know me with a few words in a letter.

I don't know if age matters but just for statistics, I'm thirty-one years old with brown hair and hazel green eyes. I've always been athletic. I care about the environment. I'm a vegetarian. I love being outdoors. I love the work I do but it's very draining - probably because I haven't figured out how to balance giving to others and giving to myself.

I work in the bodywork field incorporating mind, body and spirit. Officially, I have a master's degree in Physical Therapy but do non-traditional PT work.

Although my work is important, I feel people (friends and family) are the most important. I hope to hear from you if you feel so moved.

Love, Light and all things beautiful,

Laurel

Driving back from the post office, I was excited yet apprehensive. What a long shot - to write an intensely personal letter from only a few words in a paper. I wondered if I'd get a response.

Chapter 12

Almost Home

There must be the generating force of love behind every effort destined to be successful.

-Henry David Thoreau

Within seven days, I received a return letter from #34279. I looked at my name on the envelope several times. I was amazed at how much the handwritten response looked like my own. I read with great anticipation.

Dear Laurel,

Might I start by giving a name to a number. My name is Byron. It's interesting to note that I too have been alone for almost a year and have a longing for companionship. Not that I mind my solitude, for being alone is a self-reflecting process and much of human understanding comes from internal awareness.

I am of no structured religious orientation. I guess if I had to describe my spiritual philosophy, I'd say it to be Eastern in nature. Throughout my life - in work, in relationships, in my solitude, and in my lifestyle - I've pursued truth, not the absolute, but the actual and that, of course, is not a stagnant process.

I live a simple lifestyle from long ago. I've learned to separate my wants from my needs. Financially, I've never been in want and although I am not wealthy, I've been richly blessed in many ways.

I believe in pure water, pure air and pure food. Yet in this tainted world, compromise is a necessity. I have an active interest in human nutrition and health as well as the science of biological agriculture.

Some of my employees describe me as earthy and I guess that's a valid observation. Literally, my livelihood comes from the sun, soil and water. I am in the business of horticulture. I like the horticultural work but the business is a pain at times. But both must go together to make a living. I am career-oriented which can have its downside. Those of us who are successful (however that's measured) generally devote ourselves to our life's work.

I grew up in a family with an agrarian and horticultural background, who encouraged natural foods and a lot of contact with the earth. My parents were environmentally minded as far back as I can remember. My father had a keen interest in alternative lifestyles and organic farming. My outlook and ideals were greatly influenced by my upbringing.

I often use the theory of karma in my explanation of life's relationships, not to bring understanding to the moment, which is where life really is, but to explain the overall joys and struggles of our close relationships. In some way, for me, karma has explained the hardships as well as the blessings that life brings us.

Of course, who I am can never be put into print. Yet, I hope this gives you a little more understanding than a few words in a newspaper. There's a bit of a story behind that.

I must say describing myself in writing has been an interesting exercise to say the least. Hope it didn't seem too inward but that is where all of life emanates from. To borrow your phrase, "I hope to hear from you if you feel so moved." I must say that you and your friend seem familiar in some way and your letter did seem to touch me.

Respectfully,

Byron

The same gentle energy exuded from this letter as the original ad, but with a greater sense of knowing. I felt a distinct familiarity also, as if he were a kindred spirit.

How could words move me so quickly into emotions? I felt a stirring deep within my depths. Who was this man? He had given me his home address. I'm glad he left out his telephone number. I wasn't ready to call him. I wasn't ready to make this man come alive yet. I took out my pen and wrote back.

Two weeks went by and I hadn't heard from him. My heart was breaking, yet, I didn't even know this man. My second letter elaborated about my near-death experience and all the psychic changes I had experienced since then. I guess my perspective must have been too overwhelming and turned him off.

I turned my attention to Winnie with tears in my eyes and gave her a big hug. How grateful I was to have an animal friend, but I realized I needed someone to hug me and hold me.

I carried Winnie down the stairs and left her in the front lawn happily digging for acorns. I trudged down the last steps to the mailbox. Mail from Voluntown to Danielson would take two days to get there and two days to return. If Byron was interested at all, he would have written a letter back within one day. That was a total of five days, I reasoned. Fourteen days had past and I hadn't heard a word from him.

I hesitantly peered into the dark cavity. A few nondescript letters and then another letter with my handwriting. The letter was addressed to Byron Martin and had a big green pointing hand stamped on it. "Return to sender - Insufficient postage," the ink message read.

Why did I need extra postage on a regular letter? I wondered. I looked in the upper right-hand corner. I didn't have any postage on the letter. In my excitement to write a prompt reply, I had forgotten to stamp the letter.

I was relieved. Maybe he was still interested. Yet, if I was so grief-stricken, he must be wondering also. He had been waiting longer than fourteen days for a return. My heart went out to this man. He didn't need any more disappointment in his life. He had been in a long term relationship and was trying to trust women again.

The thought crossed my mind that this must be a sign from the universe to let the relationship go. But I couldn't walk away, not yet. I had to set this new development straight. I would hand deliver the letter the next day before work.

I drove to the Danielson post office and asked where Byron Martin lived.

"He lives on the same street as his business, Logee's Greenhouses. Everyone knows where that is," said the plump, middle-aged postman.

"Could you tell me how to get there, please?"

"Sure, I'd be happy to," he said with a twinkle in his eye.

I matched the house number to the address on the letter. I nervously pulled into the driveway of the two-story quaint looking cape-style house. It didn't look like anyone was home. I was relieved. I inspected the layout. A front door led out to a porch and a back sliding glass door entrance was near the garage. I wasn't sure which door was the main thoroughfare. Sometimes people never use their front door. I heard a neighbor's dog bark, warning me to leave. In his letter, Byron seemed liked an up front, honest guy, so he must be a front door user, I illogically thought. I stuck the letter in the front door.

I drove away with wonder, excitement and concern. All morning at work, I wondered if he would find the letter. Would the wind blow it away? Would someone else dislodge his mail or open it up? By late afternoon, I couldn't stand the suspense. I had to make sure he found my letter. I called information and got the phone number for Logee's Greenhouses.

"Hello. Does Byron Martin work there?"

"Yes," the voice answered. "Would you like to speak with him?"

"Oh - no," I said. My heart pounded. "But could you please give him an important message?"

"Okay. But I can easily connect you."

My breath caught in my throat, "No," I sputtered. "Thank you anyway. Tell him he has a letter stuck in his front door at home."

I felt better. Now, it was out of my hands. Either he'll respond or he won't, but whatever happened, I felt good about straightening out the mishap.

Two days later, I received a phone call from Byron. Our conversation was brief and to the point. We were nervous but managed to set a time to meet. I had read when meeting someone new, especially from a personal ad, to always meet in a neutral place. The most ideal condition was to have other people around if you needed help or wanted to ditch the guy.

Forgetting all that good advice, I offered to meet him at his house. We scheduled our meeting for Friday, December 11th, almost two and a half months since I read his endearing ad.

The day before our scheduled meeting, I had the first signs of bronchitis. I was working too long and hard and besides the chronic pain, I was exhausted. I didn't know if I could handle meeting someone in this condition. My only solace was I had the support of the universe which prompted me forward. "He'll have to meet me as I am," I thought.

I left work early Friday afternoon. I needed time to compose myself and rest after my work day. The drain of working with sick people all day repeatedly zapped my energy. I didn't bother getting dressed up. I didn't wear the occasional makeup I sometimes indulged in. I wanted no false pretenses.

Winnie wasn't around to comfort me. She was at the veterinarian for the weekend getting neutered. I was on my own. As I pulled out of my driveway, snow lightly collected on the windshield. I didn't have a television, so I didn't know the weather forecast.

I had second thoughts on my drive over to Byron's house. I wasn't feeling well. I was driving thirty minutes to Danielson in a snowstorm. My car wasn't reliable, and I didn't know this man. But the same compelling force that I had felt when writing the first letter, was the same compelling force gently nudging me forward now. I let all my worries peel off me with each successive mile.

By the time I arrived in Danielson, I was feeling more confident. I parked my car in front of a new gray Chevy pickup truck. I went to the door, took a deep breath and lightly tapped the antique brass oval knocker. As he opened the door, we greeted each other with a smile. His dark brown ponytail neatly tied back, accentuated his dimples and magnetic green eyes.

He showed me the depths of his being with one look. I gratefully drank his gentle, generous warmth. In that moment, a knowing so deep within me stirred, as if awakening from a long, lazy slumber. There was a recognition of our souls. This was what my older sister, Gwen, had always talked about, "if you're destined to be together, you will know instantly with one look."

I knew instantly that Byron was a part of me and our meeting was orchestrated on levels beyond our conscious awareness. Being in his presence and looking into his eyes registered a homecoming. A part of me had come home. I was overwhelmed with emotion and gratitude.

I took off my Peruvian wool cape and said, "I feel like I know you. Can I give you a hug?"

Without any words, we embraced. And as we pulled apart, we knew this was just the beginning of an incredible, powerful journey together.

The evening progressed with an honest sharing of our lives. He confessed his employees put the ad in the paper and he was grateful to them, especially after he had received my letter. Our conversation flowed as if we were floating through the magical corridors of heaven. In each other, we had found the missing key of an intricate lock that only meant something when used together. Every spoken word had meaning. Every look we exchanged, captured the essence of the other. Every movement was synchronized long before it happened. We were given a rare gift of viewing each other's divinity in a three-dimensional world. Our absorption and fascination with each other pre-empted dinner. Instead we shared the nectar of our developing love with a glass of sweet organic carrot juice and the promise of our journey over a cup of herbal tea.

During the next two months, our love was shared at the soul level. We talked about living together and getting married. The additional energy cultivated from our growing relationship was healing us on all levels. Byron, who also had chronic health problems, was improving. I completed my work days with less pain.

However, after a blissful weekend together, I wasn't prepared for my body's reaction. I went to work and did my usual protocol. While treating a patient, I experienced an acute episode of adhesional pulling in my abdomen. I couldn't finish the session and had to have another therapist take over. I went home, hoping this was only a flare-up, similar to the one in South Dakota. After two days of constant pain and pulling, I called my surgeon, Dr. Samms. He wanted to run tests and put me on pain killers and muscle relaxers. I agreed.

Byron took me to Dr. Samms office. He told me my options, "If the tests come back negative, like they usually do for scar tissue, the only alternative is to open you up and take a look inside."

I had been down that road so many times before. After the test results, Dr. Samms recommended surgery. He suspected that scar tissue was involved with my intestines, causing a partial restriction.

There had to be another way. Byron and I discussed alternative healing methods. We were committed to seeking out other means of healing after this next surgery so I wouldn't have to go through another one.

I was discouraged and disappointed with my limited sight. Just when my life seemed to be turning around, my body was unable to support me. I knew better than to blame my body. In my work, I encouraged people to honor their bodies and see what message their body brought them. I had also learned from therapy to take responsibility for my actions. As I thought back over the past year, I realized I had been receiving many physical symptoms from my body, telling me to slow down. I hadn't paid attention to these signs and now I was in a medical crisis. I needed immediate medical attention.

With the love and support of Byron and my family, I entered into another corrective abdominal surgery. I wondered what my future health would hold. But behind the wondering was determination to find a cure for an "incurable" condition.

Chapter 13

Another Detour

Although the world is full of suffering,
it is full also of the overcoming of it.

-Helen Keller

Inherent to life itself is suffering,
with suffering comes great meaning,
with meaning comes freedom.

- Methuselah

Winnie and I moved in with Byron a week before I was scheduled for surgery. I quit my job since I knew I would need more than the usual six to eight weeks to recover. Each successive surgery took its toll on my body. This operation turned out to be no different and tested my strength and endurance more.

During the operation, besides the surgical release of my twisted intestines which were stuck to my abdominal wall, I also picked up an E. Coli infection. Recovery was slow and difficult. The E. Coli bug attacked my intestinal tract and resulted in vomiting and diarrhea for two weeks. I was only out of the hospital one week when my condition worsened. I was taken to the emergency room for dehydration. Again, Western medicine seemed to have its downside. I was prescribed medication to cure the infection, but the infection had to run its course.

I supported my condition with alternative therapies. While I was recovering, Carol Allwell came to the house and treated me with acupuncture. She worked on the depleted energy meridians of my body. Byron had nutritional knowledge and put me on vitamin and mineral supplements. My homeopathic doctor prescribed certain home remedies. A Chinese herbalist from Boston prescribed Chinese herbs. I accompanied my mother and father to Florida for a month to recover in the sun which was the best prescription for me.

Although I didn't like being away from Byron or Winnie, it was my mother whom I needed most. She took care of me, like she had so many times before. She cooked, cleaned, did my wash, boiled the Chinese herbs, and burned moxie on my acupuncture meridians.

She, too, in her own way, had been through just as much as I had. Being the observer was no easy task. Often she had demonstrated her unconditional love and willingness to help. I was fortunate to have a loving mother and grateful to the universe for blessing me with her support.

I returned to Connecticut, and found that Winnie had passed over. My brother and his two kids were taking care of her, when one day she laid down on their deck and died. She was a small pig for her age. The vet said she died from congenital heart failure which was typical the way these pigs were bred. I was overwhelmed with grief. I hadn't said goodbye. Winnie had come into my life when I needed a friend. She left this world as if her mission were complete. She brought me to Byron, my soul mate. I would be forever grateful to Winnie but I missed her and cried over our separation.

I was still weak and chronically fatigued, but ready to live life again. Three months after surgery, I opened my own healing practice. I treated clients out of "Byron's home" (I wasn't ready to call it "our home" yet). I began slowly, treating only one or two clients a day. My practice grew quickly and I found I had to limit myself to five clients a day.

My healing, although slow, was progressing. Byron's emotional as well as financial support helped me explore many avenues. We felt a driving need to not only seek out alternative therapies but to also seek out spiritual teachers. We thought we would find all the answers we had been looking for. As we later learned, the answers aren't always what one expects and the seeking takes one further away from that place of knowing.

The next six months we delved into many practices. We sent away for information from the World Health Research Foundation to find a solution for scar tissue formation. There was none. We studied the Edgar Cayce readings and gleaned the information on the use of castor oil packs to soften scar tissue. The castor oil packs were effective to some degree.

We read "Alternatives," a newsletter about health and healing and discovered Dr. William Lane and his therapeutic use of shark cartilage for cancer. The brand name "shark cartilade" when taken internally in the form of a pill, cuts off the blood supply to the cancer cells. We thought that the same effect was possible for reducing the growth of scar tissue. Although research pointed to an effective use for cancer, I didn't achieve the same results.

Deepak Chopra's, ayurvedic medicine was our next avenue. We traveled to Lancaster, Massachusetts to the Maharishi Ayurvedic Center. After a thorough examination, I didn't receive any profound insights. We already meditated twice a day which was their main prescription for healing. We followed the ayurvedic way for three months and enjoyed the regimen. We massaged each other with sesame oil every night, incorporated yoga and ate local seasonal food. We drank Vatta or Pitta tea (prescribed for our body type), sipped on hot water throughout the day, and ate ghee (clarified butter). We let the program dwindle when we didn't notice any improvements.

As a result of my last surgery, my immune system was depleted. I was diagnosed with systemic candida, chronic fatigue and felt scar tissue pulling my insides once again. As was typical, the last surgery didn't cure anything, but instead bought me time to find another way before I got into a crisis again.

Dr. Byron, my naturopathic physician, prescribed treatment for the candida (yeast infections). Besides a rigid eating program, I took many nutritional supplements and homeopathic remedies to overcome the physical symptoms.

During the course of the alternative therapies which focused on the physical aspect of healing, I attended workshops to delve into the spiritual aspect of healing. I had taken many classes developed by Doctor Upledger for my physical therapy work which incorporated mind/body therapy. The most recent class I attended was Visceral Manipulation. The viscera or abdominal organs are theorized to be held in dysfunction not only from an organic cause but from an underlying emotional cause as well. For example, if someone favored their posture to the right side of their body, the liver could be implicated. The liver would not only be holding that person's body in poor posture, but the liver could also represent an underlying anger.

I learned the techniques but did not have the work done to me because I was recovering from my last surgery. I did not feel comfortable with people practicing on me, especially since many of my organs were not in the normal places. Also, since each organ represented a different emotion, I had a hard time believing that I needed to work through all my emotions, since all my organs were implicated. I found the techniques to be powerful but there was more to healing than just the emotional component.

The first healer Byron and I checked out was Barbara Brennan, author of *Hands of Light*. She had a school in Long Island, New York, for people interested in energy healing. Byron went to the Thursday evening talk with me and I attended the four day introductory course. She taught us about the human energy field and energy cords we unconsciously attach to others and allow others to attach to us. The work was interesting and insightful but I didn't feel like she was my next teacher.

By the end of August, my practice was going along full steam, yet my health wasn't improving tremendously. I received visceral treatment and did some Barbara Brennan techniques on myself but I was exhausted. I went to Maine for a long weekend with my sister, Gwen and my friend, Gail to rest. One night while sitting in the living room in front of the fireplace, I felt a presence. I looked at Gwen and Gail. They also felt a presence in the room. I moved to a chair opposite from where we felt the presence and asked who it was.

Wills' spirit came back to talk with Gwen through me and Gail was the witness. I answered questions that Gwen asked silently. I sat with my eyes closed and let his wisdom come forth:

I never meant to hurt you by leaving the earth plane when you were so young. You see, I've had other work to complete in the spirit planes before I return to your world again. My return is rapidly approaching. You too must be ready. When you look at the night sky and see all the stars twinkling, know I am smiling upon you and have always been with you, protecting and guiding you.

Next, health instructions were given to Gwen to help relieve her right ovarian pain that she had been suffering with for months. Wills said he was relaying the information from the source of universal knowledge that is available to everyone. By morning, Gwen was out of pain and had a brightness in her being. I think she had been watching the stars all night.

I felt rested when I returned home. Byron noticed a difference in me. I shared with him the experience we had with Wills. He said, "It's either Maine or your experience with Wills that is healing you because you look much better."

I told him I felt a deep peace after that experience and rested comfortably all night. Maybe developing my connection with the other side would help with my healing.

The search for spiritual teachers continued. Byron and I attended a lecture by Reverend Rosalyn Bruyere. She was another healer who also worked with energy healing and had a similar approach as Barbara Brennan. Rosalyn, however, encouraged us to embrace our humanness and our sexuality. I liked that approach. She was a down-to-earth, common sense healer. However, she wasn't our next teacher.

In between searching for healers, I was getting severe signs of adhesional pulling again. I called Dr. Samms and told him my symptoms. The scar tissue had attached to my ureter, which is the tube from the kidney to the bladder. Every thirty minutes, I'd get a tug, causing urinary urgency. Eight months had passed since the last surgery and I was approaching another crisis. I was willing to do anything for healing to avoid another surgery.

In early October, we went to view another energy healer. He was a medical doctor but was not as well known as the others. He said life comes down to conscious awareness. With energy awareness, one can heal anything. His approach was intriguing. We decided to pursue this further and attended a six-day workshop. I asked myself during an energy healing, "Why do I need to hold on to the adhesions?" The answer that came to me from my body was astounding. "It's the only way we know how to keep you here on this earth plane."

I knew I had a deep yearning to go home, back to the light, but I didn't realize my yearning was sabotaging my health. I was beginning to understand. Being in a physical body required physical attention. Most of the time, I ignored my body and pushed it until a medical crisis developed. The adhesions were a sticky-like substance holding everything together. That was one way to get me to "stick" around.

I was waiting for a dramatic cure from pain with my new awareness but nothing physically shifted. Although, energetically, I felt different. I felt more love for myself and compassion for all my physical vehicle's suffering.

Many of the healers spoke about "energy templates" which are theorized to be blueprints of one's physical body. If one changes the energy templates in a positive way, then physical health will follow. Maybe I was working on my energy templates. I couldn't get any worse for doing this type of healing and something was bound to work, I reasoned.

I knew patience was an ingredient for healing. Yet, in our fast-paced society, I wanted instant gratification, especially since my urinary urgency was so demanding. One evening, on my many trips to the downstairs bathroom, I was startled as I walked past the bookcase in the dining room. A book had fallen off the shelf at my feet and I felt a distinct presence. I picked the old dusty book up and noticed the title, *Commentaries on Living* by J. Krishnamurti. I hadn't read much by Krishnamurti but I knew he was Byron's father's favorite author. Byron's father had passed over twenty-two years ago. I asked out loud, "Are you from the light?" I received a "yes," so I relaxed, and sleepily, at three o'clock in the morning, forgot about it. These strange occurrences happened often and I had learned long ago there was nothing to fear.

I climbed back upstairs and opened the bedroom door. To my delight and surprise, the room was flooded with golden angelic light, similar to the same light in my near-death experience. I glided across the floor into the warm, loving light. I could see the outline of the window in the distance and the silhouette of the four-poster bed. I propped myself up in bed and awakened Byron. He didn't see anything but felt a presence. I closed my eyes and let the words come through.

Greetings, my children. I am happy to connect with you. I have been waiting for the moment when you would be most receptive to our communication. I am known as Elijah in the spirit planes but was your father, Ernest, in my last incarnation. I have been closely watching and guiding you for a very long time my son.

I paused, opened my eyes and saw the golden light caress Byron. His eyes filled with tears. He didn't ask any questions out loud, yet the answers were coming.

At three o'clock in the morning, your logical mind is quiet and your receptive, intuitive mind is active, that is why we have chosen to connect with you at this time. We are happy to see you are meditating, for when you are in that restful, alert state, our connection with you strengthens.

No, do not be concerned with how to meditate or whose meditation technique to follow, you have all the knowing inside. Most important is that you allow time each day to sit quietly and go inward.

Yes, we understand your health concerns. Although we cannot tell you what to do, we can encourage you to follow your inner knowing. We encourage you to take outside advice or influences into your heart and see if another authority resonates with you or not. One may. One may not. You must decide and we will support you in any way that we can.

The communication continued for over an hour. We talked about all aspects of our life, of our meeting, of our soul connection, and our "twin flame" union. The communication ended this way:

We are here for you at anytime, All you need to do is
ask and we will be happy to communicate with you again.
Hello to your mother and brother. They will come to their
own knowing, in their own time. All you can do for them or
for anyone is to live your life by example. We leave you in
peace and gentleness.

We were each touched in our own way. Byron spent the next two weeks between the emotions of joy and sorrow; joy for the reconnection with his father and sorrow for the twenty-two years without any contact. I felt waves of gratitude and the same deep peace and healing energy circulate throughout my body as I had in Maine.

After the communication, Byron and I felt an intense love so deep for each other that we wept with joy in each other's arms. Our "twin flame" connection was explained as a union of great love. Everyone has a "twin flame" or soul love. A "twin flame" is your partner for eternity. Like identical twins, we had come from the same source and were a part of one another.

During the next couple of weeks, we had many more questions. Who was the "we" that Elijah referred to? What's the difference between guidance, information and knowing? Who will our next teacher be? How do we make contact again? Do we have an ascended master working with us?

That evening, at the dinner table, I said, "Byron, let's make it simple. We'll just ask what we are supposed to do next. I want to meet our ascended master."

To our surprise, in our evening meditation, I met Methuselah. He appeared to me in a visual and auditory form. He was a bearded Biblical looking character, old and wise. His communication was informative.

I am Methuselah, an ascended master, a universal spirit guide and the steward of your spirit family. You have met me before. I was one of the many spirits surrounding and greeting you in your near-death experience. I was also at the sacred crater in Arizona, encouraging you to "Be patient."

Together, Elijah and I will be sending you much information about our world and your world. Since your visit to our side, we have developed a direct connection with you.

This information will not be for everyone. Do not worry about the opinions of others. Some may judge it harshly; others will be sparked to develop their own connection. We are only here to send you and others the greatest vibration of love and encouragement for your own development in a gentle and harmonious way. As we told Byron, living by example with the purest intentions of love is all that is necessary.

We have waited until now - until you had accepted your past experience. Now that you have honored and recognized your visit to our planes and you have asked for more guidance, we are able to connect with you further. We leave you in peace and gentleness.

I was amazed at the communication and found myself constantly questioning the truth and validity of such information. Who was Methuselah? I looked up his name in the Bible. According to the Old Testament, Methuselah, was the oldest living man on record. He lived to be nine-hundred sixty-nine years old. I chuckled. "They have a sense of humor. I've always had this secret death wish to go on to the next world. Yet, Methuselah, the man, spent many years embracing his humanness."

I wasn't convinced that our next teachers were to be in the spirit form. Wouldn't a physical teacher be easier to communicate with and believe in? Until we knew for sure, we would take a few more energy courses next summer with the medical doctor and also keep our lines of communication open with the other side.

December was approaching. Byron and I planned to marry on the magical island of Maui, Hawaii, on the anniversary of our meeting one year ago. Although my health was in a precarious position with fatigue and adhesional pulling, against my doctor's wishes, we kept the plans for our trip. I would rest on the beach, while Byron collected new plants for his business.

The plane trip to Hawaii from Connecticut was tedious, but once we landed in Maui, everything changed. The warm trade winds, the smell of fresh pineapple and papaya and the volcanic views were enough to heal anyone, especially those of us coming from a cold New England winter.

We dowsed a map of Maui to find a place to get married. The pendulum landed a few inches below Haleakala Crater, a well-known energy center in the metaphysical community. Two days later, amongst the tropical and exotic plants at Kula Botanic Gardens, we took our sacred vows.

My brother, John and his girlfriend flew out from California to be with us. Stanley and Carol North, whom we had met at one of our energy workshops, happened to be in Maui, so they came too. The wedding was small and simple with great meaning and encouragement from the other side. They were happy to support our marriage, and the "reverberations of our spiritual union were long awaited." I wasn't sure what that meant but was happy to have the blessings from our spiritual guides. Byron and I had come home within each other, enveloped in the fortitude of our love, yet I still needed healing to bring my life into complete balance.

On our return, I went to my gynecologist to see if she had any insight into my chronic yeast infections and urinary symptoms. A week later, she called. She told me I needed to come in for a biopsy because I was in precancerous stages of the cervix. I was devastated. I knew my immune system was weakened from the last surgery and I had been working too hard, but why did I have to go through any more health trials? Amidst all the blessings of our marriage and our connection with the other side, I found myself in another health crisis. What else could I do? What other avenues could I try? My body had my attention. I was ready to fight, especially with the threat of cancer looming on my horizon.

Chapter 14

Home

The first peace, which is the most important,
is that which comes within the souls of people
when they realize their relationship,
their oneness, with the universe and all its powers, and when they realize
that at the center
of the universe dwells the Great Spirit,
and that this center is really everywhere,
it is within each of us.

-Black Elk

The biopsy results told me I was two stages below a case of full blown cancer. The good news was that the abnormal cells were only on the cervix and not in the endocervical canal. My doctor recommended surgery the following week. I declined. I told her I wanted to try alternative methods for at least six months. She wasn't pleased and warned me of the risks and seriousness of my choice. She said, "The surgery is a very simple procedure and by waiting, you could throw yourself into a life-threatening situation. Cervical cancer does not have a high survival rate unless treated early."

I told her, "I understand my choices. I choose to try alternative methods for healing first." I didn't feel comfortable with a "simple procedure," especially since my health trials began with a "simple procedure." But I also understood that I was taking a risk. Risks were part of living. I'd rather risk than sit back and give away my power blindly. Byron and I discussed our options. I agreed that I would go back to the doctor in six months and have another biopsy to see if my cells had normalized.

The "other side" continued to bring me information and encouragement for healing. I was encouraged to take antioxidants and colloidal silver, a natural anti-bacterial and anti-fungal compound. I had many energy healing sessions with Byron and Gail. I started a nutritional healing program with a doctor from Vermont. She prescribed high doses of minerals and vitamins to normalize the cells. I drank Essiac, an anti-cancer tea, and took many immune system boosting remedies.

I slowly cut down on my healing practice and by mid March told all my clients I was taking four months off for my own healing. My urinary urgency wasn't any better and my chronic fatigue increased. I was depressed and discouraged. Some days I could only get out of bed for three hours but I never had more than thirty minutes of rest because I would be in the bathroom. No wonder I was fatigued. I recognized my rebel attitude toward Western medicine. I knew I had gone to the extreme of self-healing and had ignored medical advice. After a meditation, the following message came through:

> *Everything in your plane is divine, including allopathic medicine. To turn your back on Western medicine is only working with part of God's creation. You don't have to prove anything to anyone. You don't have to document your natural healing. The most important criteria is that you feel better and allow the universal flow of energy to heal you.*

In May, I went for a follow-up biopsy, ready to deal with the news. I got the results a week later. Nothing had changed. I was disappointed. I felt I had failed. I had not only let down myself, Byron and my family but my spiritual guidance. I felt sorry for myself and needed time to contemplate my chronic condition of adhesions and this new development with my cervix. I drove to Beavertail, Rhode Island, one of my favorite spots to think and be alone with nature.

To my surprise, I met a disabled seagull in the parking lot. He stood on his left leg. His right leg hung limply by his side. I looked at him for a moment, perplexed by his stare. I walked down the rocks to the ocean and found a little nook that jutted out into the sea, protected from the wind and hidden from the parking lot. I let the peace wash over me, like a wave caressing my soul. Today the sea wasn't as violent as it sometimes was against these rocky cliffs. I had no choice but to immerse myself in the day.

In the distance, I saw only one seagull. The disabled bird stared at me, permeating my thoughts:

We all have injuries yet we keep going.

He slowly ascended into the air. He flew over one rock, then another, until he landed five feet from me. Even with a strong head wind, he landed perfectly. Gracefully balanced on one leg, he never felt sorry for himself. Instead, he hoped to eat a few morsels from my salad.

This grand gull was my teacher and encouraged me to test him. I threw a tasty crouton in front of his beak. He didn't hurry to snatch it. He let the wind tumble it down onto a lower rock. As I thought about climbing down to retrieve this tidbit of food for him, he turned his head, looked straight at me and said,

Watch - I'm a very able bird. I've learned to function and live with all of my challenges.

Again he displayed winged mastery. He captured his prize and landed closer, into a tucked resting position at the base of my feet. As the gull and I shared the rock, feeling the early afternoon sun penetrate our hearts, I heard his wisdom once more:

We all have challenges in life. We can meet these challenges head on and learn from them. Or we can sit on the edge of a cliff with a hopeless, helpless perspective. We may not fly the same, walk the same or eat the same way again, but we can still live life to its fullest - just in a different way. And when we learn to embrace whatever we face, then we are living by example.

I wrote the last words in my journal while my seagull sage squawked in confirmation. He fearlessly flew a sweeping pass in front of my eyes. I watched him soar into the sunlight and was struck by his parting wisdom -

Never give up hope!

I tried to catch one more glimpse of him. He was lost in the glaring light. Instead, I saw his final gift - a magnificent rainbow, completely circling the sun!

I had started the day feeling weighted down with decisions and unsure about my future, but by the time I left Beavertail, I was elated. I felt a renewal of hope. I could meet any challenge. My husband, my family and my spiritual guidance weren't let down. I was doing the best I could and I had all the support I needed. My disabled seagull reminded me to count all my blessings, to keep a positive attitude and never give up hope. I realized no one was disappointed in me but myself. I didn't have the luxury of disappointment. Whatever that meant for me, I was going to live my life, day by day, to the fullest. If I needed to have surgery I would and I would support my surgery with alternative and complementary therapies.

I realized I felt guilty for not overcoming my illness. I was buying into the "new age" thought of "creating your own reality." What a ludicrous position. I believed in taking responsibility for one's actions but I needed love and nurturing, not guilt and blame. I had berated myself for my weakness. I asked Elijah and Methuselah for their perspective. They replied:

> *Greetings my child, you are concerned... concerned about suffering and struggle and abuse for what you and others have been through. Have you created your own reality? You ask how and why?*
>
> *First, let us begin our discussion with compassion and gentleness. Most everyone acknowledges some form of suffering and those who don't, are not yet ready. However, as we have said before "Inherent to life itself is suffering..." therefore, every human being has experienced some form of suffering to a greater or lesser degree than others. Yet, there is the first uncompassionate act... for one man's suffering cannot be compared to another man's suffering. Yet one man's suffering is everyone else's suffering.*
>
> *When you move into that place of oneness, everyone else's pain is your pain, their struggle is your struggle and their suffering is your suffering. However, when you move into that place of oneness through compassion, everyone else's pain, struggle and suffering ends because you are one. You completely understand and honor their choices because they're your choices too!*

I was confused. "How does one obtain oneness through compassion?" They replied:

Compassion and love for oneself is a place to begin. We encourage you to look at your being, your body, and your soul with compassion and know you have done exactly what you needed to do, given your circumstances. Allow the space in your being to be free of past, present and future judgments. And if you judge, allow space for that too. You see, my child, you are honoring yourself for all that you have been through and for all that you are. That includes the judgment, the hatred, the anger, the grief, the guilt and the rage. It includes the confusion and the disappointment. Allow room for who you are as the first compassionate act.

When you make space for all those feelings and acknowledge them, then you can let them go. Let them go back to the light. Let the light transmute them into compassion and love for yourself. Fill your new spaces with as much love and compassion as your being can handle.

Gentleness is also part of the process. Allow feelings and emotions to surface when they are ready. You have different needs with different time capacities. For some, awareness and letting go can happen in an instant. For others, awareness may take years and the letting go, years later. Faster is not better. Everyone's process is different. Be gentle with yourself. There is no prize for arriving at the gates of heaven first or for comparing your accomplishments to others. Comparison is again putting you back into separation. Our side is more interested in oneness, love, peace and harmony.

Others may choose to let go of their pain and suffering and never have to recall their traumatic events.

Everyone's healing is different but there's a common thread - everyone needs healing.

Whether you consider your healing to be major or minor, physical, mental, emotional or spiritual, it's all the same. When you discover compassion and love in yourself, you will also discover this in others.

The abundance of love and compassion will let you experience joy, ecstasy and creation to its fullest. And you still ask "Why do things happen the way they do?"

Do you know your logical mind will never get a satisfactory answer? Seeking the answer doesn't heal you but wears on you. It robs your energy and increases your frustration and slips you back into judgment and out of compassion.

Know when you ask "why" from a place of love and compassion, the answer looks much different. Ask yourself, "Can one see the big picture with blinders on? If one with limited vision and limited senses knew what was lurking around the corner, would one choose that path? Would one create that reality?"

From a limited point of view, the compassionate presence in yourself, will answer, "no." Yet with a broader view, an unlimited range of senses and a knowledge of divine order, the answers may be different if you understand your soul's purpose.

Continuing a discussion about "creating your own reality" when one has limited perception only brings up feelings of guilt, responsibility and victimization. One loses sight of one's innate compassionate presence.

A soul incarnates for many reasons - one being growth. Challenges are needed to bring about that growth. However, in a free will environment such as earth, these challenges can and have turned into major traumas. From a compassionate perspective, you would not say you chose to make minor challenges into major obstacles. We encourage you to discern the information given by those who insinuate you have chosen your hardship. On a greater soul level, your divine presence is not here to encourage your demise but instead to lift you up.

When you overcome major obstacles or are living through them, what a magnificent light you hold and carry. You may not be aware of your radiance. You have such a profound message and gift to share with others. Your suffering has great meaning and once you discover that meaning for yourself, you'll find freedom. Freedom from the pain, freedom from the struggle, freedom from the suffering...and with that freedom comes oneness and your way back "home."

Go in peace and gentleness.

I was beginning to understand. I needed to embrace all parts of my being and find meaning in my suffering to go home - home to myself. The first embracing I did was to accept that I needed to balance traditional medicine with alternative medicine. I scheduled the surgery for the beginning of July, after Byron and I returned from another energy workshop.

We went to the workshop in Sedona, Arizona with a new perspective. We embraced our path and acknowledged that it was different from others. From my knowing and communication with Elijah and Methuselah, I understood that one person wasn't more enlightened or better than another.

Attending the workshop brought a different perspective and contradicted my inner knowing. Everyone talked about initiation levels of light, discussed who carried more light, who saw more clairvoyantly, who created their illness, or who was the best healer. I witnessed a group of people more interested in division and separation than unity and love. And although love was talked about, I rarely found it demonstrated.

The methods and the workshop didn't resonate with my being, but the enticement for enlightenment (whatever that was) hooked us. I learned from the experience to always go with my inner knowing and not let outside influences persuade me. Some people needed a group, a teacher and validation for their spiritual path. We also looked for validation but found it within. And our spiritual teachers were from the "other side."

I questioned why we had attended this workshop and discovered the reason by the end of the workshop. I spoke to Annette, an instructor at the course, who had healed herself from cancer. She had worked with me during the session and knew my health history. She attributed much of her healing to the Philippine faith healers. She encouraged Byron and me to experience the power of the healers for ourselves in September when she would be sponsoring a healer to come to the United States. We were excited to try this new form of healing, but first I was scheduled for surgery.

I went home and got a second opinion from Dr. Karrs. She did a complete workup and said I could have laser surgery, a less drastic procedure than what the first doctor had proposed. I agreed and had the surgery in July. Within a week's time, I felt better. I welcomed assistance from traditional medicine. I could now put my energies into building my immune system, overcoming candida, and releasing the scar tissue pain.

In September, Byron and I traveled back to Arizona and had four days of healing with Brother Jose Segundo. On each of us, he performed two psychic surgeries a day. Psychic surgery is an energy technique that penetrates one's energy body and physical body. No anesthesia is used, yet there is no pain. Brother Segundo, a short, dark-skinned Filipino, with a broad smile, worked with cleansing the blood and clearing the energy field. Like many other healers we had learned from, he said all disease is carried in the energy body. If you heal the energy body and reorganize the templates, then the disease will also be healed.

Byron and I went into the session together, so we could witness each other's process. As I lay on the table, I noticed a single white candle burning and a picture of Jesus Christ on the wall. The feeling in the room was one of warmth and trust. He attributed his healing gift to the Christ energy. I told him nothing about my health history and instead concentrated on being willing and open.

His words in broken English surprised me. "How long you have cancer?"

I was shocked, I couldn't say anything so Byron answered. "She doesn't have cancer but had a precancerous condition a few months ago."

They continued to talk, as if I wasn't in the room, "She needs Philippine ants for next three months. Healing power of ants will cleanse her energy body of the cancer."

After the first session, I was overwhelmed with emotion. The powerful energy that jolted me was like an electrical shock without the consequences of the voltage. I was grateful for the opportunity to experience this dynamic phenomenon. Over the next few sessions, Brother Jose worked on cleansing my blood of any remaining cancer cells. He also worked on the adhesions, which he termed "deposits of tissue, sticking my insides together."

He encouraged Byron and me to travel to the Philippines to learn more about psychic surgery and get more treatments. In Brother Jose's estimation, my condition was "complex and needed much work to realign the energy bodies." Byron also received healing.

Until we could decide about the Philippines, I ate Philippine ants every morning. I followed a non-acidic diet which included avoiding tomatoes, citrus fruit, vinegar, shellfish and dairy products. Any animal or animal byproduct that would have eaten the ants while alive was cut from my diet. I banished chicken and eggs. My immune system felt revved up, my candida was subsiding but I still experienced urinary urgency from the adhesional pulling.

Byron and I decided to go to the Philippines for healing. Financially, the trip would be less expensive than paying for another major surgery in the hospital. All of my medical expenses were "out of pocket" since I wasn't able to get any kind of health insurance because of my existing condition. And although I would incorporate Western treatment if necessary, first, we would immerse ourselves with the Philippine healers.

On the last day of October, I traveled to the Philippines. Byron would join me later. On this trip, I was accompanied by Carol, the woman who had attended our wedding almost one year ago. She was a breast cancer survivor but now had a new development. She had liver cancer and needed immediate attention.

Carol, a bright blue-eyed, petite woman with blonde shoulder-length, braided hair, was one of those people for whom you would do anything, although she rarely asked for anything. I realized what a privilege I had been given when she did ask. I was not only going to the Philippines for my own healing; I was also going to witness the healing of a fellow traveler.

After twelve hours in the air, we were only halfway to the Philippines, so we decided to deplane and lay over in Hawaii for a night. We were in the Hawaiian sun resting, when Carol told me about her Slavic ancestors. She spoke candidly about her mortality. "I'm either going to make it or I'm not, but either way, I'm going to go on with glory" and in the same breath she laughed and said, "But the one thing I don't want to do is die with any money in the bank."

We fantasized how we could spend money and have a good time doing it. We played that day doing somersaults and handstands in the ocean. We embraced and celebrated life and our upcoming journey.

When we arrived in Manila, I was shocked at the filth, poverty and pollution. When I looked at the multitudes of people, I felt their desperation. My heart went out to them with compassion and understanding. When I looked at them as other souls, I saw a simple beauty.

We went to Baguio City, the summer capital of the Philippines, about two-hundred fifty kilometers north of Manila with an altitude of one-thousand five-hundred meters above the sea. The rainy season had ended and we were greeted with mild temperatures. The weather reminded me of an Indian summer's day in New England. Most of the faith healers lived in Baguio and had clinics where they treated the sick.

After resting from our three days of travel connections and adjusting to a thirteen hour time zone difference, we began our healings. Like everything else in my life, I approached my healings with zealous excessiveness. Carol did not. She had a different agenda. I saw eight different healers. Although I started out having two healings a day, by the time Byron arrived, he and I received between ten to twelve treatments a day.

I worked with a local healer, Brother William "Willie" Nonog, every morning for four hours. I not only witnessed over one-thousand healings, I was directly involved in their process. Willie was a gentle sort and was considered the "local doctor." His energy was pure and bright. He had done healings since he was nine years old and had great humility about his gift. He attributed his healing abilities to the universe, the "God Source" and the Christ energy. His clientele consisted of Filipinos with a few foreigners, like Carol and me, sprinkled in between. He operated solely on a donation basis, many times receiving fresh vegetables or rice from the local community.

After two weeks, Carol moved in with Willie, his wife, Shirley and their three sons. Carol had grown weak from the traveling and didn't have the strength to ride back and forth from town. She also wanted to approach her healing gently. Willie was her main healer. I was experimenting with all the healers in town and stayed at a local hotel so I could come and go as I pleased.

Carol and I shared our lives together for a brief moment in time. I was getting stronger. Carol was getting weaker. The weekend before Byron arrived, Carol mustered the last of her strength and we went to the beach. As we walked along the South China sea at sunset, I asked Carol "What is your passion in life? What keeps you here?"

She said she didn't have any passion. Yet as I thought about our times together, I was aware that she didn't have to have a passion because she lived life passionately. She ate papaya passionately. She danced passionately. She followed world news and politics passionately. She approached her healing passionately, on her terms.

As we spent more time together, Carol became more inquisitive about death. She asked about my near-death experience. After I shared my story, she said, "I won't have to worry about you shedding any tears over death. It's like you are my angel sent from heaven to guide me on this trip." I was touched. But I felt Carol was my guide. She taught me about compassion. I wanted to help cheer Carol on to healing, but I learned healing didn't always mean living. Carol was healing into death. I was healing into life. All I could do was support Carol's transition.

While Carol struggled, my health dramatically shifted. Byron and I received treatments from one of the most flamboyant and well-known healers in the Philippines. Jun Labo was an aggressive and graphic Filipino healer. He was married to Yuko, a Japanese woman who also performed healings. He had a clinic in Baguio and treated many foreigners, including a large population of Japanese people. But his clinic was mostly known for treating the desperately sick. We had spoken with Jun the day before and he had given us valuable insight about the healings. He said, "Whenever you are on the healing table, connect to your higher source, ask for all the negativity to be released and ask for divine grace."

He also said, "The trouble with illness is that I can shift the energy fields and bring people into balance and wellness, but if they go home and live in the same pattern, then the disease comes back."

This particular sunny day in late November, Byron and I contemplated what Jun had said. As I lay on Yuko's healing table, I asked for all the adhesional pulling in my abdomen and especially around my bladder to be released. At that moment, I opened my eyes and saw Yuko removing scar tissue from my bladder area. Instantly, I had no more urinary urgency, pain or pulling. I was overwhelmed with emotion. After almost one year, I was out of the critical stages of scar tissue restriction. Over the next two weeks, Byron and I returned regularly and by the end of our treatments I was completely free from pain. I had been living with chronic pain for twelve years. I had, in part, found that "Holy Grail."

I also received confirmation from all the healers that I didn't have any remaining cancer in my energy field. I was relieved. Medical tests, three weeks later, verified that my abnormal cells had normalized. I knew Jun's second statement was important too, "...don't go back to the same pattern of living before your illness." I was committed to changing my life when I got home so I could stay well.

After approximately one hundred psychic operations each, Byron and I left the Philippines. We were in good health, in good spirits and had high hopes for our future. Carol chose to stay in the Philippines for more treatments. I felt confused. Why had Byron and I received profound healings and Carol wasn't getting physically better? I realized Carol was healing, just in a different way. Her spirit was brighter. Her knowing was clearer. She embraced her path. She wasn't upset that she was dying, she had work to do in the spiritual world. She regretted leaving her husband but lovingly knew he would find his way.

When I learned of Carol's passing, I cried. My tears were mixed like the first sleeting rain in early spring. For as many tears of joy I shed for her freedom, I had as many tears of sadness for being left without my physical friend. And although I had been to the other side, I learned one can have knowing and still have tears and one can have compassion and still have tears.

In retrospect, I realized that with the chronological unfolding of our trip, Carol also shared the chronological unfolding of her life. It was as if she was having, what many near-death experiencers call, a "life review" before she passed over. Carol told me when I got home to watch one of her all time favorite movies *Zorba the Greek* with Anthony Quinn. Little did I know, her passing would coincide with my viewing the film. I finally understood. She wanted to either live in glory or pass over in glory. Carol did both.

Carol's passing reminded us of our state of separation, of the suffering inherent in life itself, of the meaning found in suffering and of the freedom that awaits us. There is a place in us that yearned to be with her, with the light and return to "Source" as she had done. I felt for others too, knowing everyone she had touched in her life, had gone through similar thoughts and reflections and discoveries. Everyone had experienced and learned from her passing in their own, unique way - whether to grieve or rejoice or just be.

Our trip home from the Philippines was joyous. We laid over in Maui, Hawaii for a week to rest. Our stop was filled with reflection, contemplation, gratitude and love. The past year had brought us many challenges and gifts. Our path was different than anyone else's. After many alternative therapies, we learned one was not superior to another. My healing came from a combination of allopathic medicine, alternative medicine, and universal knowledge. We learned to follow our inner knowing and higher guidance which allowed us to map out our own unique prescription for healing.

We would go home and change our patterns. I would go home and work with my hands through my true love of writing, not with hands-on-healing. Byron would go home and reorganize his business. With renewed hope in our health and well-being, we discussed the possibilities of children. We welcomed an opportunity to share our love with another soul. Although a pregnancy for me was considered risky (according to allopathic medicine), we felt enough healing had taken place to allow us to try.

During our last evening on the island, we drove to dinner in our rented Pontiac convertible, feeling the tropical breezes caress us. We never thought we'd be back in one year's time to the magical Island of Maui celebrating our anniversary and our health. We stopped the car at a park on Haleakala highway. As we walked hand-in-hand, viewing the Hawaiian sunset, I looked into Byron's green eyes. With traces of light reflected from his depths, I said, "I've come home, Love. There wasn't any magic formula. There wasn't any place to go. I've learned 'home' is embracing my humanness, living in the here and now. 'Home' is my love for you and your love for me."

And with tears in my eyes, I continued, "I've learned 'home' is my support system of family, friends and spiritual guidance. 'Home' is aligning myself with my true spiritual nature. And most importantly, home is within each of us, allowing us to bring the 'light' into every day living, trusting we have a purpose, even though at times we cannot see that purpose."

With the last flickers of sunlight, we embraced and kissed as if all of time throughout the ages had been collected into this one moment. We were honoring each other's place in the universe, knowing that "anything is possible" with hope, faith and love.

PART II: Universal Messages

Introduction

Most journeys begin before death, my journey began after death. When I was clinically dead and traveled to the "light," I was in the presence of many spiritual beings. Upon returning from my near-death experience, a series of events unfolded as I have described in Part I.

One of those events was my communication with the other side. While my personal journey evolved, over thirty messages were written and inspired in part, by whom I perceive to be universal spirit guides. I have included twelve of these timeless topics in Part II. Each topic was and is relevant to my life's path. I hope these messages will enhance your personal pursuit.

A Message From the Guides

Greetings to all seekers of truth. Our names are Elijah and Methuselah. We are universal spirit guides and are happy to share this information with you. Please allow the words to openly reach that place in you that knows. A unique message awaits each one of you. If some of the information presented in the following pages does not "resonate," then know it was not intended for you at this moment. With each reading, increased clarity, understanding and depth will uplift you.

All the knowledge in the universe has been interpreted before, in many different ways. Everyone has access to this information. We encourage you to strengthen your connection to our side for guidance, clarity, love and support. Death or near-death is not a requirement to unveil your inner wisdom or resources greater than yourself. Willingness and an open heart are all that will be needed. Begin by allowing your first thought about any decisions in life to blossom. When you give that "intuitive" hunch permission to come forth, you begin to align yourself with your true spiritual nature.

You see, my children, all of you are greater than your three-dimensional selves. Some call this expanded being your soul, higher self, angelic self, godself, star seed or spirit. Align yourself with whatever is comfortable. When you tap into your greater being, you become a receptacle for information. Guidance and messages from the universe will come your way. Again the term "universe" can be substituted for God, Buddha, Christ, Source, All-Knowing or whatever fits your background.

We encourage living within the universal flow to bring you joy and ease. With these writings, we encourage you to feel them in your heart, glean the information you desire and leave the rest.

Please be in no hurry, for what is time? What is of the essence?

Go in peace and gentleness,
-Elijah & Methuselah

Chapter 15

Love

I had met my true love, Byron Martin, and everything was great in my life. I had a successful healing practice and I was pursuing self-growth work. Outwardly life looked wonderful. But, I was working too hard. I facilitated other's healings to the extent of ignoring my own health. Inwardly, my body reacted. I was in precancerous stages of the cervix and had scar tissue complications from my operations. One day while contemplating my situation, this communication about love was written.

Love

What is love?

The most powerful force in the universe is love. Love is an expansive, yet simple, topic. Everything and everyone needs love.

Love is the fuel that runs the body. In the automobile, the quality of gas affects all parts of the engine. In the body, higher octane love affects all parts of your being - the physical, mental, emotional and spiritual bodies. Kerosene and conditional love have one thing in common. They paralyze free-flowing movement.

The deepest yearning inside of you needs love. That unfulfilled part of you needs love. The answers you search for are love. The purest love is found in your light body, your energetic body or spirit body - when all you are is pure essence, pure energy and pure love. There are no limits. There are no boundaries. You are boundless and limitless. You are all-knowing.

Close your eyes and feel your power, your essence, your greatness and your oneness. All of these are love. For being in the place of love, being "in love" is all there is. Love heals all, cures all, nourishes all and feeds all.

Every action done in love, from the place of love, is the greatest of all. The immensity of love, the power of love is recognizable. When you live your life from the place of love, you realize your potential. You tap into your purest state.

Traditional thought has one loving others at the expense of oneself. Love's fullest potential begins with loving yourself first, unconditionally. Yet when you love yourself without judgment, the more you are able to love others in the same way. When you judge yourself, you also judge others and take away from loving yourself and others. When you love yourself and others, you add to love and make room for abundant love. Love makes decisions easier. Ask yourself, "What's the most loving act I can do for myself?" When you act lovingly towards yourself, you also act out of love for others.

Everyday, upon waking and before sleeping, say a loving thought to yourself. For example, "I love you skin. Thank you for supporting me and protecting me," or, "I love my emotion of fear. Thank you for alerting me to stay present and attentive when I feel conflict." Your body needs to hear that you love it. Your emotions need to hear that you love them. Your spouse, lover, children, cats, dogs and plants need love. The more you tell yourself out loud that you are in love with you, the more you can tell others that you love them too. The words at first may not seem sincere but with practice they will gain depth. The vibrations of these words carry energy into higher realms and many levels. This love will come back to you magnified in many ways.

The simplicity of love is that "love just is." Love is. Love has no definition, no label, only experience. Defining love puts restrictions on love and compartmentalizes love. Love is free-flowing. To know love, one must feel love. Love is the first bloom of yellow crocuses along a sand-covered sidewalk in early spring. Love is the first ray of sunshine, highlighting a spider's web, dripping with morning dew. Love is the smell of garden soil as you dig in the earth to prepare for broccoli plantings. Love is the wind-burned face and sun-streaked hair that twinkles back at you from the mirror. Love is. Love just is.

Try this exercise. Picture or imagine what or whom is the most dear to you in this life. Let all your feelings and emotions well up inside. Remember or imagine a moment when you were deeply touched by this other person or thing (ie: nature, animal). Then stop and hold that feeling and picture yourself in that other person or thing. See your face. Keep sending and holding love, joy and bliss. You have experienced self-love. Self-love is present whenever you give love to another. And when you love yourself first, the love given to another is known. Love is merely a reflection of you. You are loving yourself.

Try this same exercise with a partner. Send them love. Hold them in the highest esteem. Look at your partner, eye-to-eye. Cherish their being. Honor their soul. Applaud their courageous journey. Then signal each other (by squeezing hands or nodding heads) and hold all those feelings. As you continue to look at your partner, let their eyes become your eyes, their face become your face, and their journey become your journey. Take your time. Enjoy, relax and feel. When you need a boost about loving, repeat this exercise.

Everyone has experienced divine love. Divine Love is where you came from. Divine Love is where you will return. You are not separate from divine love. You have divine love inside you and outside you. You are surrounded by and filled with this love. At times you are unaware of love. You have forgotten. We are here to help you remember your divinity. We encourage you to strip away old fears and beliefs and allow the love that is.

Love is...
Spiraling low
Spiraling high
Divinity is...
There's no divide.

Above
Below
Around we go
Until we stop
To let love
Flow.

Receiving a perspective on love, brought home the message about self-love. When I asked, "What is the most loving act I can do for myself?" I received my answer, "Close your practice and heal yourself first." After struggling with many issues (ie: money, job title, worthiness), I followed my inner knowing and closed my practice. Loving myself became my full-time job. My health improved. My relationship with Byron changed. We lovingly met our own needs and had great understanding for the other. Together we experienced the expansive, yet simple, power of love.

Chapter 16

Fear

Byron and I were preparing to travel to Arizona to experience the work of a Philippine healer. We had fears and concerns of the impending situation. As a business owner, Byron was concerned about wasted time and money. Would his business survive without him? Would the money we spent on the trip be rewarding? I was afraid of the healings. Would they hurt? Was I a candidate for healing? Were the skills of the Philippine healer a hoax?

Fear

What is fear?

Fear is similar to darkness. Fear is facing the unknown with a lack of information and a lack of knowing. As F.D.R. said "There is nothing to fear, but fear itself." Yet, fear makes people forget. You have forgotten that you are all one and the spark of divinity is inside.

Many believe in separation. With the illusion of separation comes fear. Fear can come in the form of scarcity, mortality, abandonment, or impoverishment. Fear can stem from addiction, losing control, pain, isolation and lack of love. If you accept the illusion of separation, you accept fear because you live with attachments to separation.

We encourage you to look at your life through the eyes of oneness. You are a part of everything and everything is a part of you. Everything and everyone is an aspect of yourself. Fear, separation and attachment are temporary. When you pass over to our side fear, separation or attachment do not exist. You might experience a "death" in your mind only and move into oneness while you are living. When you become unattached to things such as money, sex, security or your physical body and experience detachment, then you free yourself to move into a limitless supply of abundance, unity and love.

Fear prevents abundance. To experience abundance, you must be willing to let go of everything. You do not need to live a meager lifestyle and donate all your earthly belongings to charity, unless you so choose. We are encouraging you to become unattached to outcome and allow yourself to live freely and abundantly in the moment, unencumbered by worry and concern. As our friend Emmanuel says, "Worry is a lack of trust in the divine plan." Worry is also an aspect of fear that drains your energy and keeps you in separation.

When you move into a unity consciousness of love, you move yourself in the direction of confronting your fears. Next time you worry, ask yourself, "What is it that I fear at a core level?" Go into the fear. See if the fear gives you information. You may receive information about an aspect of yourself. You may find that you fear, fear itself, and by approaching it, you diffuse it.

Byron and I confronted our fears and traveled to Arizona. Byron allowed his business to operate without him. Upon our return, he discovered areas of his business which needed improvement. By spending money and not attaching an outcome to our trip, we moved out of the scarcity and impoverishment consciousness. I entered into the healings with an awareness of surrender, knowing whatever was supposed to happen would. The healings were not painful. And the Philippine healer did not consider psychic surgery a skill but a gift from the divine. He did not charge money for his gift but donations were given. He considered himself a vessel for healing and the outcome, whether one healed, was not in his hands.

Chapter 17

Emotions

Growing up with three brothers and two sisters, I was the tomboy of the group. My emotional state at the end of my formative years was unbalanced. I was comfortable with anger but not with sadness or tears. I had learned to endure pain and not be a "crybaby." Once I started psychotherapy, I saw how off center I was. Psychotherapy got me in touch with my feelings but I was terrified of emotions. This communication comforted me.

Emotions

Why are some emotions good and some bad?

Emotions are neither good nor bad. These are only labels. Emotions are an avenue of expression in the form of feelings. Emotions connect you to your heart, your spirit and other people. Everything elicits an emotion. Emotions are an expressive and expansive energy. Emotions give you that charge for the battery.

As we discuss emotions, read this with an open and feeling heart. Heavy emotions may seem dark, especially if "feeling" is a new state of being. Like a full moon glowing in the darkness, your emotions will illuminate the way. As the night passes, so will your emotions. You will awaken with keen awareness to the breaking of a new day.

Emotions are cleansing. Emotions are healing. Like the balance of yin and yang, emotions such as joy and sadness, laughter and crying, or ecstasy and despair can be experienced simultaneously. Think of a life experience where you've had sadness and joy interlaced. For example, when a dear friend has suffered before "dying," you may experience great sadness at this loss and great joy for your friend who now has freedom from pain. The emotion of despair may surface because you are left with unanswered questions. Despair turns to ecstasy knowing you will one day find freedom, be reunited with your friend, have all your questions answered and return to oneness.

Emotions give you an opportunity to open and experience your humanity in a beautiful, wonderful way. Every thought and action has an emotional component. Developing your awareness, and expanding your emotions, will bring you joy. You may experience pain with your emotions. We encourage you to go into the pain through your emotions. Many times through the pain, you will experience joy. At times you may feel that the pain is too great. Honor that feeling. Give yourself permission to take a break from the emotional pain. When you are ready to experience your feelings, those emotions will surface again.

Emotions may also cause pain if you fear being emotional. Fear puts distance between you and your emotions and therefore you back away from them. When you back away, you encourage separation, which is the root of fear. When you are in an emotional state, your mind loses control. Encourage your mind to give up control. Let your heart orchestrate your emotions.

Trust and surrender to your heart and you will move into spontaneous emotion and into a "feeling" state. Staying in your mind only frustrates your emotions. Many are numb to emotions and automatically label and categorize their surroundings. Your natural world is a wonderful place to experiment with emotions. Next time you see a flower, don't identify it with labels (ie: This is a red rose). Instead, be with the flower and feel it. Feel the energy from the flower. Let the fragrance penetrate all your senses. Let the gift of the flower's life force reach your heart center. Do this exercise with a pet or a person. Feel their life force, their vitality. Look beyond their physical shell. Go into their eyes, into their heart. Hug them. You may feel lots of emotions or sense an energy. Whatever you experience is right for you.

Emotions need to be nurtured, loved and cared for like a young child. Accept them without judgment. If a toddler knocks a glass off the table by accident, don't yell and be angry at the child. Toddlers are uncoordinated and spontaneous. They are living in a form natural for their age. Your emotions may become like the toddler, unpredictable and spontaneous. Yet, when you encourage your emotions or your toddler to interact with the world, then you open the "avenue of expression."

However, emotions, like toddlers, are sometimes not ready to express themselves. Time is not important. Emotions and toddlers will express themselves when they are ready. Encourage kindness, gentleness and reverence, without judgment and comparison - allowing a safe environment for expression.

Emotions are in the world for you to experiment with and experience. All feelings are worthy. Allow yourself to be whomever you are in this moment. When you embrace all parts of your being, you experience the emotion of love - the most powerful force in the universe.

I experienced my emotions with less fear. When I felt sad, I cried. When I felt happy, I laughed. And when I hit my lowest points of despair, contemplating taking my own life, I waited it out. I found joy through the pain when I allowed emotional spontaneity. I continue to practice "letting go" so I can be whomever I need to be in this moment.

Chapter 18

Healing

I went to the Philippines with my friend Carol. We were receiving treatments from the Philippine healers. Carol, who had liver cancer, didn't seem to be getting better. On the other hand, I was getting stronger everyday. I was confused about healing. Why are some healed and others are not?

Healing

Is healing truly possible?

Everything is possible, including healing yourself and facilitating healing in others. Healing is a matter of aligning yourself with the purest intentions, highest vibrational light and allowing your true spiritual nature to flood your being with its essence. Healing comes with hope, faith and love. All healing comes from within and a source greater than yourself.

When you sincerely ask for divine healing, you shall receive healing. However, healing does not always come in the way you might expect. For example, healing does not always mean living. Regardless of the ideas around death, death is in itself a great healer. Death is a welcome transition for the sick. The blessings that occur when one passes over are tremendous and many times, outweigh the prospect of living with limitations.

Each soul has a choice about life and death, yet most are unaware of this proposition. Have you chosen to be with the living in physical form or the living in spirit form? If you choose to heal into life and stay in physical form, one must explore the possibility of circumstantial change. When one receives healing, one must alter his or her life situation or the illness will return. Change can come in all forms. Change may be great or small, internal or external, but always includes the realignment of thought.

Sometimes change occurs and the illness still returns. This pattern of reoccurrence may be part of the soul's path. Either deeper layers are being healed or this person's illness is serving as a great teacher for self and others. The soul may decide the challenge is too great for its personality and reevaluation occurs.

Have you ever been with someone who was ill? They know if they are going to live or die. Some may choose to return to spirit. Take your cues from the person preparing for transition. Are they accepting or are they fearful? Have they resolved their life issues? Are they giving cues about preparing for a journey? They will beautifully heal into life at death. The outcome of living is not important at the soul level. However, to friends and family the outcome is essential. Yet the odds of dying are one out of one. Therefore, living moment by moment and staying in the process is all there is. When you can encourage or assist another to heal, don't be attached to outcome. Instead, celebrate their courageous journey in whatever form it takes.

Stand firm in your knowing, trust in the divine plan, and live momentarily, knowing that everything is possible.

I gained clarity about healing. I healed into life. Carol healed into death. I remained in physical form. Carol made the transition to spirit form. Carol taught me about the preciousness of life. She also taught me compassion. I was attached to the outcome of physical healing until I witnessed Carol's preparation for her own passing. She healed beautifully into death while I stayed here to tell her story.

Chapter 19

Health & Wellness

Byron and I were vacationing in Maine at my grandparent's lake house. I was recovering from a post-surgical infection. Soaking up the sun's healing rays on the dock, I looked up toward the house. A familiar scene unfolded. Gramp, age eighty-six, was on his hands and knees, weeding his petunia bed amongst the tall, white birch trees. His wife Murm, age eighty-seven, was by his side as she had been for sixty-one years of their married life. They were happy and healthy and I wondered what their secret was?

Health and Wellness

If one experiences health, does one also experience wellness?

Health and wellness are issues for many. Everyone has or will face their own health and wellness. Health and wellness have different definitions, perceptions and standards. The most important idea is your own.

The man, like your grandfather, who eats ice cream everyday, enjoys working in his yard, smiles at the world and laughs with his family is experiencing health and wellness on all levels. Conversely, the man who complains about his food, curses the weather, despises his family, and appalls his body is living without health and wellness.

All of life is perspective. Focusing on what you have instead of what you don't have, lifts you from pain and misery to health and wellness. Greeting life with innocent curiosity and bubbling excitement, energizes you to live in health and wellness. The outcome of perfect health is no longer the focus and by ending the seeking, you arrive.

Look toward elders who are happy and content. Notice how they embrace each day with wonder and joy. They have accepted life and live in the moment. Your elders also consider life "a mystery," and don't spend unnecessary time and energy to answer why. They develop a liberating wisdom of knowing that they don't know. Age is not a requirement to gain wisdom. In these rapidly changing times, we encourage you to fully embrace life now with all its mystery. Your wisdom will awaken and allow you to accept that part of you which doesn't know and a greater part of you that knows all.

Health and wellness are not meant to be a struggle or something to be achieved. Effort alone moves one further away from what is desired. Health and wellness are an allowing and unfolding of your greater being. Allowing life to evolve instead of forcing life to happen encourages your body's natural process to take over.

Life is unnatural when filled with self-judgment. Self-judgment is harsh, unyielding and detrimental to one's well being. Sending messages such as hate, dissatisfaction and guilt, also sends messages of pain, unworthiness and struggle. Many of you have unconsciously sent these types of messages to yourself. Gently ask for awareness of your thoughts and you will see how often you send self-judging messages. Awareness is the first step to changing the message.

Self-judging any action, sends lower vibrational messages on an energetic and physical level to yourself. These self-judgments can manifest into disease. Repeated judgment made by others can also be harmful if you allow the words to enter your consciousness. Removing yourself from others' opinions is one way to heal.

Children cannot always remove themselves from others' judgment. Children growing up in abusive households are inundated with lower vibratory messages. Patterns such as low self-esteem and self-worth will extend into adulthood. Time, effort, awareness and love are needed to reverse these patterns.

Messages of hope, love, and encouragement are high vibratory messages. Children receiving these messages can transcend the lower vibratory messages of others in adulthood. Also these adults don't send as many self-judgments.

Regardless of your upbringing, you are all divine beings and worthy of health and wellness if you so choose. Some have learned to function in dysfunction and change is a frightening prospect. Yet, the only permanence in life is change. We encourage those who need encouragement.

Many times perfectionistic tendencies develop which will damage your health and wellness. If you set your standards on perfection, then you strive toward a self-imposed goal. We suggest that there is no need to strive for perfection. From our perspective, everything and everyone is already perfect. Loving yourself and your world with all its "imperfections" moves you into perfection.*

*See Addendum - Divine Order, page 187

When you continue to send your body messages of "not good enough" or continue to put more pressure on yourself to achieve and perform, you will continue to find yourself out of balance and disharmonious with your surroundings. Perfection accepts the universe "as is." Perfection does not have you change the universe to the way you think it ought to be. Accepting divine order encourages you to effortlessly change by embracing your world non-judgmentally with all its perfect "imperfections."

Health and wellness is not a drug store prescription, a nutritional program or a daily meditation. Health and wellness is a matter of perspective. How you view your life and how you view your interaction with the universe gives you perspective.

If you are ill now, you are most likely working through a greater awareness. Disease brings you to new places of discovery within yourself. There is no need to feel guilty with illness. Ill health is a great teacher and encourages you to take a closer look at yourself. Courage is needed to look honestly at oneself and remain non-judgmentally in compassion.

Disease gives you an opportunity to be in touch with your body, feeling all its aches and pains. You are in the magnificent process of tuning into your body and cleansing it of all the toxins. Your body is wise and knows how to get well. Listen to what your body needs. Practice giving your body positive messages. Practice self-love and compassion.

When you continue to allow and trust, you radiate much light. When you radiate much light, your vibrations *change. When this light strikes your physical being, some-times you experience pain. Pain is not always a bad thing. Sometimes pain is part of the healing. When your vibrations change, you are healing your physical vehicle as well as your soul.*

I was relieved after this communication. I relaxed and stopped trying to become well. Although, I didn't always understand "divine order," I trusted that my soul was perfectly orchestrating my health and wellness. I accepted the pain as a good feeling, knowing I was healing.

I looked toward Murm and Gramp. They were living in the moment with the petunias, with each other and with their family. That was their secret - staying present in the moment and appreciating each day as a gift. Being in their company encouraged and inspired my tired body and inquisitive mind.

Chapter 20

Paths and Practices

I was searching for a way to get back to the light - "searching for home." Although I understood "home" was within each one of us, I wanted someone to tell me how to find home. Byron and I had met many spiritual teachers, all of whom had their own belief systems. We were confused about following someone else's path or practice.

Paths and Practices

Is there a path or a practice that will bring me closer to the light?

A common illusion in your world is that a path or practice will bring you closer to the light or show you the way home. The mind that wants to know feeds that illusion. Proof is needed and a concise, logical road map from point A to point B is desired. Finding a path is a creation of your three dimensional world.

The only path is no path at all. When one follows a path, the path never ends and becomes the path of infinity which again is no path at all. We encourage each of you to guide yourself, moment-by-moment. Many of you who are accomplished or goal-oriented are easy prey for those selling an active way to the light. Have we mentioned that currency doesn't have value on our side? Divinity isn't for sale. Divinity is a gift waiting to be completely unwrapped.

All paths and practices, like all things in your world, have their perfect place. One path or practice is not better than another. If you understand, then we applaud you. You have found the fruits of many "ripe" teachings.

With an open heart, everything in life, that is the way of the light, will come to you naturally and beautifully. The progressive fragrance of a pink peony in late spring, blossoms naturally with care and attention. Care and attention to oneself will allow you to blossom in the same way.

If you need to label your efforts as a "path" or "practice," then keep it exclusively as your own. People may want to follow or lead. We encourage you to develop your own way. When you stand alone in a field of wheat, yet together with all the grain, this allows you to live your own life in a healthy, vibrant way. Together, yet alone, the golden grain sways in the melodious wind.

Some stalks of wheat will come to full growth, others will not. Most will be harvested, others replanted. Several will grow tall and healthy, others will be swept up into the infinite world of the beyond. What a grand day for the grain that grew with its own direction!

You each have the ability to grow on your own. Although you are a part of the collective, you are also individuals. The strength of the many, comes from the few. Many draw strength, hope and inspiration from individuals honoring themselves and living by example.

We encourage you to relax into the moment, honor what is for your highest good, and go with the universal flow. Nothing needs to be figured out. There is no path or practice to seek or to follow. Only joy, lightness and love are in store for you. You may, however, choose to lead or follow along a path which may be exactly what you need for your highest and best good.

Whatever you choose will be perfect for you. If your choice is difficult and leads you to struggle, you will learn how to change. With a deeper understanding, Your spirit will guide you back home. If you are in question and doubt, we suggest you go inside, through meditation, prayer or simply breathing. Allow your inner knowing without judgment to come forth. Path and practice are not words to be avoided. Instead look at your intention behind the words. For example: Is your meditation a rigid prescribed practice or does meditation, allow you to enjoy a deeper connection to yourself and our world? Are you locked into a certain way of meditating because that's how it's supposed to be done? Or have you developed your own natural flow?

Paths and practices have been especially needed in your turbulent times, for they have given comfort and stability. For those of you who need to feel action and only feel connected when you are seeking, honor that too. Let your decision to continue a path or practice come from your heart. If your concern is "I will be less 'spiritual' because I'm not doing anything," ask yourself what does "spiritual" mean and ask who is judging you. Is it yourself? If so, acknowledge that part of you and allow your preconceived ideas of spirituality to drop away like the cocoon of the transforming butterfly ready for ascension.

Coming to a knowing is not in doing but in being - in being human!

I hesitated to share this communication because of the nature of the message. "We are not to follow another and take someone else's word or path but find our own way." And there lies the paradox - but here's how I understood paths and practices.

I had tried many different practices. I learned from different teachers but I was not cut out to be a devotee. I honored others for their places. And understood, what was right for me was not necessarily right for another. I was happy to have confirmation to follow my "own" path and not to consider my life a path but just a place of being. Understanding life as a pathless land freed my energy to live more consciously in the moment. I stopped searching for home and thus found home.

Chapter 21

Enlightenment

Byron and I attended many energy workshops in search of healing. We met a variety of people who talked about enlightenment via levels of initiations. According to some groups, after you've attained your fifth initiation, you're considered an enlightened being. To me, enlightenment meant someone who emanated love, generosity and humility. I found being "enlightened" didn't guarantee such qualities. Instead, initiations became a competition which only served to separate and divide. I was confused about enlightenment.

Enlightenment

What is enlightenment?

Enlightenment is the ability to hold and carry more light.

What is light?

Light is energy. Dark is energy. Everything is energy. The difference is that light has a different energy than dark. Light is informed. Light knows. Dark is uninformed and doesn't know. One needs light to be in knowing and understanding. Ultimately, light unified with love is the most powerful.

Are light and love the same?

When the energy of light is experienced in the heart, one feels love. The pure essence of light is experienced as love on our side. In a near-death experience, an encounter with the light is interpreted as an encounter with unconditional love. When pure essence meets pure essence, without boundaries and blockages, oneness is experienced. The purity, perfection and fusion of oneness is love.

Another common illusion in your world is that unconditional love only exists on our side. Unconditional love is experienced in your plane when light hits your core, your essence, your soul, or your pure energy of oneness.

Light is the same as love when experienced with your heart. With gratitude and humility, light can be as powerful as love and has all the transforming abilities of love. The light that you receive and uncover in yourself has an ability to expand your love for yourself and humanity.

The combination of love and light will bring about the purest kind of enlightenment. The same kind of enlightenment one reads about from the great teachers and masters such as Mother Meera, Mother Theresa, Gandhi, Krishnamurti, Christ and Buddha. With humility, love and gratitude these beings reached an "enlightened" state in the service of love. They experienced a freedom of life.

Enlightenment is different from long ago when the great teachers and masters combined the essence of love and light. Once a high state of enlightenment was achieved, their work of service would end in the earth plane and continue in the spiritual plane.

Can one reach enlightenment without love?

A state of holding more light or en-light-en-ment is possible because of the rapid planetary shifts and conscious transformations happening in your world. One can carry more light without the purity of love, yet it is love in your world that is needed the most.

Some spiritual teachers are working very hard and fast to heal your planet. They have been teaching people to carry more light and to hold greater vibrations. Mother Earth has needed healing for a long time, and those who have taken on the task of holding more light are helping in this crisis. However, to hold more light without love is only a short term solution to "buy more time." The earth's energies will stabilize with light but will strengthen and heal with love.

Enlightenment is not always, at first, love-centered. Love sometimes lags behind those who are searching for light. However, light has a high vibrational quality. Light opens doorways for love, humility, oneness and freedom. In the past, many years were spent by yogis and gurus to reach Nirvana. Time is no longer a factor. Many spiritual groups today have the ability to bring in high vibrational light and energy.

We encourage love and light simultaneously, instead of relying on a "quick fix" for yourself and your planet. Unnecessary hardship is endured for those on a "fast track." The temptation is to hurry and find enlightenment. Or, to get more light before time runs out or before someone else gets more. First, time does not run out, and secondly, light, like love, is abundant. There is a limitless supply. Planetary influences, astrological alignments, angels and spiritual guides are working with your transformation.

Initiation levels are a talked about phenomenon. The labeling only serves to separate and divide when what is needed is unity and love. How much light or love one holds need not be compared to another's. You are all divine spiritual beings with a powerful purpose. By asking during daily meditations, one can let in more light and love. Allow the energy into your heart. Feel love transform you. Let this increased love wash away old patterns. Let love develop new awareness. Feel the oneness of your humanity. Feel the universality of the light. Embrace the "All" with love. Allow suffering to be washed away. Fill the spaces with love and light and feel the freedom of enlightenment.

I quit attending energy workshops that focused on separation, division and competition. Instead, I aligned myself with unity and love. I relaxed about reaching higher states of enlightenment or labeling my process. I participated in life momentarily allowing my journey to gently unfold. I consciously stopped seeking, which allowed the abundance of love and light in the universe to come forth.

Chapter 22

Time

I was in limbo. I had given up my healing practice after having invested seven years of time and money into my education and work. My dream was to be a writer, to touch people with written words instead of with my hands. But writing was another investment of time. Intellectually, I knew that time didn't run out. During my near-death experience I had experienced a timeless state. Why was I hung up on time?

Time

What is time?

Time is a strange phenomenon in your plane. Time permeates every part of your being. When you add the complicating factor of space and lifetime after lifetime, one gets caught in a time/space continuum. Time as you know it, does not exist in our world.

Many run their lives by the clock... everything has a deadline... everything is on a schedule. A day is planned out weeks in advanced. No wonder many live in a momentary illusion. Many find the moment difficult to live in because so much is invested in time.

Time brings out a restlessness inside of you, an impatience for having things done yesterday, or a mental or physical list of what needs to be done next. Your inner drive *to strive and achieve is related to time and space. If you were not of time and space, then you would not have these feelings.*

We suggest that you throw away your watches; then you will not be looking at them wondering, waiting and expecting. You will have the opportunity to live in the moment. Of course, we understand your need for practicality with a clock in the house or office. However, we ask that you contemplate for a moment life without a schedule, without time constraints like appointments. Would the world become more relaxed? Would people follow their true nature, allowing their natural state of being to take over? Would there be fewer accidents, more patience, better health and an appreciation of living purely in the moment?

Look inside and see what drives you. Is there something you feel you have to prove or accomplish? Is it keeping up with others? Or is it the ticking clock of your "mortality?" Do you feel that time will run out?

Time is a three-dimensional quality that you place upon yourselves. Putting pressures on yourself to be the best, to get the job done first, or to achieve and succeed in a specified time frame is unnatural. When you look at life and death as natural cycles, you realize these cycles are a transformation of energy. Time assists in the transference of energy. Death will no longer drive you when you realize that time doesn't run out. Wherever you are in this present moment you are exactly where you are supposed to be. Without the constraints of time, you relax into the greater reality of living.

Become aware - aware of your struggles, aware of your daily moments, and aware of your time pressures. When you are involved in something and you constantly struggle, look at why you are struggling. What would happen if all of a sudden you said, "I'm not going to struggle any more; I'm going to find another way?" All the energy going into "struggle" would be free to flow into your life's natural path. The root cause of time pressures is fear - fear of time running out, fear of loss, fear of death. If you know that time doesn't run out and that death is another stage in the growth process, wouldn't you stay in the moment?

Time management is often linked to success. What is success? Is success how much money you accumulate in a year, how neat your house is or what kind of work you do? Without trying, some accumulate wealth, live with order and have the job they want. These people are in a timeless state, living in the flow of their spiritual alignment.

Other's struggle with survival, clutter and a job title. These people are always fighting the clock. Will the next bill get paid? When will the time be spent on cleaning out that closet? When will a fulfilling job be had? You see my children, living in abundance is everyone's true nature and if you treat time as a timeless state then things that have been put off will happen now. Now is the time.

Many of you know and some of you have experienced a timeless state beyond your three-dimensional existence. However, when you are back in your world, you become bogged down with the details of life. Ask what the details are teaching you. What can you learn from your daily tasks?

Take a step back and reprioritize your life while looking at the big picture. Each of you has a desire to return to oneness and each of you has a divine purpose. Your daily path will help you discover your divinity. Every time you reaffirm your divine purpose, your life will flow more easily and your world will become more harmonic. What matters in life is not what you thought mattered.

The most important part of your life is learning about love. The more you love yourself and accept who you are with all your humanness, the more you make room in yourself to love others. If you want to keep your watch, accept that as your true nature to need to know the time. You are honoring that part of you that needs to know. All parts of your being have a wholeness to them. By allowing different aspects of yourself to come forth, you will bring them to wholeness. Move into celebration. Celebrate the permission you have given yourself to be whomever you are, without any time constraints or pressures to be anyone else.

I stopped looking at time as an investment. Time didn't cost me anything and time couldn't be spent. I let go of the thought that I had wasted time as a physical therapist facilitating healing. And I followed my true nature and became a writer.

Some days I am in flow with time and other days I force an unnatural time schedule upon myself. I'm perplexed about my need to get things done on time, but accept it as my nature for now. I feel liberated when I stop struggling with self-imposed goals. For example, if I didn't write that chapter today, I put down the pen and delight in knowing that words are timeless. They don't demand a schedule, I do.

Chapter 23

Meditation

I had been regularly meditating for three years when Byron took an interest in my daily routine. He asked many questions. "How do I quiet my mind? How long do I meditate? What are the benefits of meditation? What's the best way to meditate?"

Although I had experimented with many techniques, my perspective was clouded from being taught "how to meditate." I was feeling confined with my meditation technique and I was having difficulty meditating when I was in pain. We received these words of encouragement to clarify what meditation was all about.

Meditation

What is meditation?

Meditation has many meanings. Much has been written about meditation. Meditation from our perspective is "allowing." Meditation allows you to go inside and outside yourself. Meditation allows awareness in a restful, alert state. Sometimes after a meditation, you wonder about your thoughts or where you were. You were in a state of awareness.

While meditating, you're aware of many levels. You're aware of your physical world outside, yet with a deepening of your state, your inner world takes precedence. Your inner world is where multidimensional knowing takes place. You may get flashes of thoughts or see pictures. Nothing makes sense to your logical mind but everything makes sense to your meditative mind. You not only give your physical body a chance to rest but you also spark and awaken your inner self to take charge of your life. From this vantage point you are "in flow" and the carry over becomes stronger in between meditations. Linear and nonlinear thoughts meld. Soon your whole life becomes a "meditation" and "in flow" becomes a natural state of being.

How does one meditate?

Meditation can happen anywhere or anytime. Walking can be a meditation. Driving a car can be a meditation. Sipping tea can be a meditation. When you are in the "allow mode," staying present and conscious to each moment, each action or each observation, you are in a meditative state. We encourage meditation in a sitting manner with your eyes closed to allow yourself to shut out your visual senses. This method drops you into a state of deep awareness. You may have a million thoughts. Observe those thoughts without judgment. You may be pulled by your thoughts. Yet like the ocean tide, dropping deeper, below the surface roughness of the waves and the wind, will put you floating in the calm and peacefulness at the bottom of the sea. Your reserves of inner peace have been reached. The pull of the tide may get your attention (which could represent a barking dog in the background). Realize at times you may be pulled up and dropped back down repeatedly. If physical aches and pains pull you out of meditation, observe them. Let the aches and pains know you will come to the surface. By acknowledging their existence from the deeper recesses, you are also sending them healing energy. With acknowledgment, the aches and pains may float away with the tide, never to return again. Or your bodily symptoms may be sending you messages for your next step in healing. Feel the calm, the peace, and the safety of the ocean floor. Feel the warmth of the rays filtering down upon you. Create your space however you would like.

Trust that every meditation is a good meditation. Allow yourself to "allow." Some find meditation is enhanced by repeating a word. Picturing the ocean tide or following your breath can also act as a repetition to assist you to deeper levels of awareness. Experiment and see what works best for you. There is no right way or wrong way to meditate. You may feel pressured by repeating a word or following your breath. Performance or achievement is not meditation. Repeating a word or following your breath once may be all that is needed.

There is no set time to meditate. Meditation allows you to free yourself from the time/space continuum and explore deeper layers and many levels. The amount of time you spend meditating is not as important as the intent to meditate. However, since you have grown up in an achievement-oriented society, the challenge is greater to let go of the time/space existence.

Yet, with meditation you will notice that the pressures of yesterday are not the same as the pressures of today. You will live more "in flow" and be comfortable to let the doors open instead of prying them open or seeking them out. Longer isn't better. Taking time to meditate is important, especially for spiritual guidance. When you are in a "meditative" state we are better able to connect with you. You are more receptive to outside guidance and inside wisdom when you take the time to meditate. You are in the "allow mode." People who don't regularly meditate will sometimes get inspiration while they are driving, or before they fall sleep. They have experienced a form of meditation, letting their minds relax, and allowing messages to come forth.

Universal information is like food dropping down through the waters to the ocean floor for the fish to eat. Fish don't go to the surface in the middle of a storm to look for food. They allow the food to come to them. Meditation allows information or inspiration to come to you.

Meditation is an effortless state of existence. There is no need to "try to meditate." Meditation reminds you of your natural flow and your true nature. Many things can happen when you meditate, or nothing at all. Whatever happens is exactly right for you.

Acknowledging your meditation as unique, transcends all the comparison and brings you into oneness. The logical self has difficulty understanding oneness; through meditation the multidimensional self understands oneness completely. Meditation, prayer, or contemplation will bring you into oneness. Many know the feeling but descriptive words lose the essence of oneness.

Many of you have experienced a brief instance of recognition and a flash of universal understanding. When you recall the experience with your logical mind, the essence of the experience is gone. When you allow a meditative state to emerge, you will experience this state of oneness over again. You understand all, because you are all.

Oneness is not a place to strive for, but a knowing that you have been there. Although you may forget, through meditation you return to oneness. Some of the meditations in which you most greatly experienced oneness were when you felt tired, your head nodding. Fatigued, your mind transcended to more elevated planes.

Trying to "quiet" your mind in meditation leads you to an active mind, encouraging you to do what you wish to stop. However, an active mind in meditation is not to be judged. Those meditations are also "enlightening." Practicing non-judgment with your meditations spills over into your daily life. You view others with a non-judgmental attitude, allowing that person to be whomever they are. When you find yourself judging your meditations, see if you are not also caught into judging others in a similar way.

Participating in your own daily meditation will open channels beyond your conscious knowing into our higher vibrational realms. Meditation is one way to embrace your higher guidance and inner wisdom. Meditation need not be a defined spiritual path or practice but a melding of momentary living. If you fear meditation, we encourage you to ask for the highest beings of light, a high level guide, your higher self or angelic self to be with you while you meditate.

When you meditate ask for patience and kindness to yourself, laughter and lightness with your world, and love and blessings from the universe and you will live with joy, ease, prosperity and abundance. Allow yourself to go, think, do, or be, in whatever state you need to be in - in that state of "being."

Byron began meditating regularly and I tailored meditation to meet my own needs. I acknowledged my physical pain that I sometimes felt during meditation and learned more about my healing process.

Every day our meditations are different. I allow my meditations freedom of structure and judgment. Although I find my meditations most restful by setting a few guidelines. I generally meditate twenty minutes in the morning, five to ten minutes at noon, and fifteen to twenty minutes in the evening. Some days I meditate for longer periods and other days, I only meditate once. However, when I meditate, my life flows better, I feel the presence of spiritual guidance and I'm more centered with my thoughts and actions.

Chapter 24

Purpose

While living in the Philippines for two months to pursue my healing, I had time for reflection. Sitting on my hotel's hillside balcony overlooking Baguio City, I watched the multitudes of people. Much like an American city, they hurried to get somewhere. I was overwhelmed thinking about universal divine order and marveled at the organized chaos. I wondered how many people were living their life's purpose, or if they even considered such a thing. Was I living my life's purpose?

Purpose

Does everyone have a purpose?

Every soul has a purpose, unique as the individual, yet in a bigger framework, you're all working toward the same common goal. One common goal is to return and reunite with "Source." When a soul departs and becomes part of the oneness, then the soul is in the unity consciousness. Living life now with the backdrop of returning to Source, allows one to live in present day unity.

There are many paths to reunite with Source. Passing over to our side is one way, but a physical death is not necessary to live in the light. We are here to guide and encourage you now. Free will choice allows you to make your own way. We encourage you to choose the way of the light, the path of the highest vibrational quality for yourselves. Every choice made from the unified perspective brings you closer to that perspective.

You see my children, your world with all its polarities has divine order. Polarities are part of that order. For example, you are all one, but that does not mean that you are all the same. Each of you is unique and individual. Like a magnificent jigsaw puzzle, each intricate piece has its place, yet unable to come to wholeness unless honored in its slotted assignment. You are all working together in a grand plan. When you heed your grand purpose, you will honor and find your daily purpose.

In living your daily or moment-by-moment purpose you are honoring your grand purpose. Your grand purpose and daily purpose work like interlocking screws of complex machinery. Discussing purpose allows these interlocking latches to be set into motion. With awareness and inquiry about your life's purpose, you will find your life changes.

Like life itself, purpose is constant change. One day your purpose may be to nurture yourself and the next day to care for an aging relative. Each task is of high quality. When you honor your highest good, then you also honor your grand purpose.

When you are spiritually aligned with your true nature, abundance will flow. Fear no longer rules. Are you working or training for something that is aligned with your spiritual nature? Does your purpose allow you to exercise freedom of your heart and soul? Or are you tied into something from fear or lack - lack of prestige, lack of title, lack of money?

Changing your life's direction in midstream concerns many. Yet, wouldn't the beaver, who got caught midstream, back paddle and change course, rather than go over his dam into downstream waterfalls? However, for some, a drastic plunge may be needed for change. And this sudden turn of events may be a blessing in disguise - that is, if one survives the waterfalls.

However, there are many opportunities to try again. Inquiring about your life's purpose sets the machinery into motion to change course. All will be shown. Surrender to the details of how, when and what. "Ask and you shall receive." Be ready to receive for the dam will break with a flood of help, guidance and assistance.

How do I find my purpose?

Purpose is not a seeking but a knowing, and may be found in the process, not the outcome. The greatest joy and harmony is in the process and encourages the outcome to become the process. How can you maximize each day and each moment? Can you become the moment?

Close your eyes after reading this paragraph, and allow all your sensations to go inside. Feel your body, your connection to the earth at your feet and your connection to the heavens at the top of your head. Go to your heart and breathe in light from heaven and earth. Allow the light to fill your body. Let all your muscles relax. Tune into your ears. What do you hear? Allow all the sounds to float in and out, and soon you will hear a music unto itself. Go to your eyes and forehead. What sensation do you see or feel? Let go and allow yourself to be transported to wherever and whatever space is needed.

When you open your eyes, take a deep breath. Thank yourself for giving you an internal experience of momentary purpose. In that moment, your purpose was to connect with everything and everyone around you. When you go about your day and seem to lose focus, we suggest you try this exercise to reconnect into the process of momentary living.

Every moment of every day has a purpose. Ask yourself, "Is this act or decision that I'm about to do, part of my purpose and process here on earth? Is it serving me, my fellow traveler, and the light of the highest vibration?" You will know in your heart, whether or not to pursue your present course of action.

Look beyond the labels. Labels do not define your purpose (i.e. healer, teacher, gardener). The thoughts and actions behind the label define your purpose. Where are your intentions? What are the intentions of others? Whose standards are you striving for? Are they your parents, your friends, the societal or collective consciousness? What's for your highest good? How are you serving others?

For example, you may meet a holy taxi driver and a greedy, manipulative healer. Both are serving others, yet one has God-like intentions while the other has God-less intentions. One may be content and happy while the other is greedily aspiring for more. Both individuals have a unique path and position. One is practicing divine grace while the other is pretending to have divine grace.

Tune into your inner knowing. Are your standards driving you to accomplish, achieve and perform? For whom, we ask? Can you see the sun will continue to rise and life will continue to repeat itself again and again and again? Lives will be born and lives will be lived. Tunes will be played and tears will be shed. When your time has come for transition, the stage will fade away. You will see, from a distance, all the acts and the scenes for your review. As your spirit lovingly reviews, you may find scenes you would like to change or polish. Or you may want to change plays completely. You will know clearly and wonder why you spent so long with one prop or one scene.

Do not judge harshly. You are learning. You may have completed your teachings. The time has come to be filled with more light and move on to your next assignment. You have free choice. You may decide to stay on our side and work as a spirit guide. Or you may choose to go back as an ascended master or teacher in the earth plane to share your oneness, love and light with others.

All choices are honorable and the way of light. Living and experiencing earthly life is part of your spiritual lesson. Choosing life is an earth bound predicament for many. You remember where you came from and realize embodiment is not always easy. However, you can change that thought and move into embracing life now. Be assured, all your choices, every moment of every day, are accumulating and preparing you for eternity. Choose wisely. If you cannot make a decision, then know it's not time to make one. However, inaction is action. If fear holds you back from progressing to your next stage of spiritual development, encourage the fear into the light. Fear is simply a lack of information and light is information.

Your purpose may be to risk a leap of faith. We encourage you to "go for it." Your risk may include a change of jobs, relationships, neighborhoods or something more internal and subtle, like viewing the world with a different perspective. Viewing the world from your heart versus your mind shows a different picture. "How can I honor myself, thereby honoring others and honoring the light?" you will soon be asking yourself.

If there has been something you've wanted to do for a long time, the time is now. There is never a "good" time, a "right" time or a "wrong" time. The more often you take a risk, the more the universe will support you. When you think the rug is being pulled out from under you, look for the beautiful hardwood floor underneath. Polish may be all that is needed.

I started viewing my life's purpose as a momentary process again. I didn't have to be a Noble Peace Prize winner, only an extraordinary ordinary person. I kept the backdrop of oneness in view but at times lost my way and got caught up in trying to figure everything out. Once I switched jobs and followed my bliss, I felt aligned with my true spiritual nature. The most joy and meaning I've found in my life is listening to others by supporting, encouraging and learning from their life's journey.

Chapter 25

Inner Kingdom

Byron and I had trouble meditating in the Philippines. We were unable to relax with all the commotion. Was it the noise, the pollution or the sight of Filipino's carrying guns on the streets? I opened the Bible in our room and the words that caught my attention were "Inner Kingdom." I wondered if this was the answer. Would focusing inward help our outward state?

Inner Kingdom

What is meant by inner kingdom?

Have you heard that "the kingdom of God is within you?" That kingdom is your kingdom and that God is your godself within. When your inner house is in order, then your outer house is in order. Outside influences take your energy away from your inner resources. When you control your outside world, you dampen your inside sanctuary. Many of you are concerned with security of wealth, safety, family and relationships. Yet, security does not exist. The collective consciousness has brought you that wonderful illusion. Striving for an idea of perfection in the outer world compromises your inner world.

Does it matter who has the neatest lawn, the most expensive car or the quietest neighborhood? Concerns with outer and worldly influences distracts one from the inner sanctuaries and inner knowing. Pay attention to the details but do not become the details. Be in the world but not of the world.

Planetary and personal healing begins in your inner kingdom. Allow the outside to become part of the inside, especially when you meditate. Your outer environment will always be filled with noise. Yet you will find that barking dogs, racing cars or blaring t.v.'s will fade away as you go deeper inside yourself. The constant buzz of outside activity will turn into an inner buzz of focus in meditation.

You see my children, when your inner kingdom is honored, your divinity unfolds, and everything else falls into place. Inner peace and sanctuary are not found in material wealth, a job title, a fast car or a racy relationship. No one can take care of your needs better than you. You are the chosen one to honor your path and your divinity.

Other people's opinions are part of your outer world and only add more clutter to your outer house. Measuring your spirituality or the amount of light you carry are judgments which are unimportant in your inner world.

When you go inside, to your inner kingdom, all the outside clutter is stripped away. Your inner kingdom is filled with purity and love. Light and the highest vibrations of knowledge await you, like a ripe apple waiting to be plucked. Your inner world will give you answers for all your questions.

Be gentle with yourself on the outside and go to the inside where gentleness lives. Treat yourself with the same reverence and care as you would a newborn's soft delicate skin. Go to your inner world of love, peace, joy and harmony.

As you stay i n the inner world, you discover you're not o f the outer world. As you continue to build and honor all your inner godself voices, and stay centered in your angelic presence, the outer world will affect you less. Yet you will have a great effect upon the world.

This concise communication brought home the message of focusing inward. I stopped listening to other people's opinion since their opinion was none of my business. Instead, I went to my inner world and imagined all the peacefulness I felt in meditation exuding outward. The effect was amazing. The external chaos took care of itself. The outside world didn't change, my perspective did.

Chapter 26

Birth, Life & Death

Byron and I recovered from our trip to the Philippines by spending a week in Hawaii. We talked about having a child. Our friend Carol who had liver cancer stayed in the Philippines. She knew she was dying. I reflected upon our different paths. We talked about birth and Carol talked about death. Life seemed so strange.

Birth, Life and Death

What's your perspective on Birth, Life and Death?

> *Birth, life and death are natural, encompassing cycles. The meaning of these cycles occupies your energy, space and time. Everything happens in cycles - the plant kingdom, the animal kingdom and the seasons of nature itself.*
>
> *The four seasons are much like your human existence. Spring begins life - a birth. The first part of summer is the maturing process. The last part of summer gives full life. Life slows down in a graceful, beautiful way in autumn as the leaves change color or turn "gray." Winter represents death.*
>
> *During the four seasons, nothing dies or comes to an end. All seasons represent a transition. During the winter months, the energy of the seeds or bulbs lies dormant, much like your spirit before its next incarnation. Your energy does*

not cease to exist. Your energy, essence or soul is in a resting phase to recharge, recalculate and reevaluate its next mission. Like in the springtime, your spirit is born to a new, yet familiar existence. Your daily life is much like summer - living life to its fullest, yet changing slightly as fall approaches. Fall represents your later years in life, where a melding and a blending of accumulated knowledge prepares you for another transition. This can be done gently and gracefully or violently, depending on the storms set into motion or the resistance one has. On a stormy night, many leaves fall to their next transition. Winter is a time for celebration as the spirit or soul is greeted by others. The soul's energy is free to discover, explore and travel in an unencumbered state like a snowball rolling down a hill - collecting more snow or energy to be brought back into a physical form.

Have you often wondered why children have so much energy? They have returned from their wintry trip and like the springtime, have abundant energy to explode with delight. If nurtured, respected and encouraged these new little beings can hold on to this universal energy for themselves and allow it to pass through them freely to others.

However, adults who have lost their vital spirit energy will dampen, drain or melt the child's energy. When the child's spirit is crushed, the child's energy is devastated even into the adult years. However, symptoms now show earlier than ever before with disorders in children such as attention deficit disorder, hyperactivity, overweight adolescents, autism, environmental allergies and hypersensitivities. Can you see what a courageous set of beings have come to your planet to teach and awaken the adults? They have come to encourage their parents to take a look at their own spiritual purpose. These beings have a hard road, yet they are some of your greatest teachers.

Also, there are beings now incarnating to already awakened parents. These souls are orchestrating with divine oneness deciding when and with whom to incarnate. More of these exciting births are happening. When an enlightened soul has chosen to come into existence with full memory and knowledge of divine oneness, the parents are challenged. They have been brought together for their last incarnation to house, prepare, encourage and support this enlightened being. The snowball will not be crushed but encouraged to collect more energy. This collected energy will be passed along to others. The enlightened souls will not only become healers and teachers for their parents but for a great number of people involved in planetary transformation.

When life is viewed as a mission or completing one's purpose, then death or transition, can be viewed as a joyous time. Being left without a friend or lover, brother, sister, mother or father can be difficult. However physical separation is part of your three-dimensional world. Yet you have the ability, with awareness, to contact and be with the person who has passed over.

Opening yourself to the spiritual world on our side can be a great healer. Do not fear transition, for you have all been here before and will return. Many loved ones are here to greet you and await your transition. Energy changes will happen as you embark upon this new, but remembered, journey. Those of you who have had a glimpse of our side are messengers to alleviate fear, worry and anxiety about death's finality. We have worked with many of you. The need is increasing to assure others. Those of you who have been here, know this place of peace, rest and knowledge.

Those who have chosen to transit to our side will, after a much needed rest and rejuvenation of their spirit, gear up for their next assignment. For those of you left in the earth plane with a spiritual knowing or understanding of our side, your transition will be one of joy and ease. Be assured you have a remembrance of our side and although you may lack a direct memory in your present lifetime, your spirit understands.

We encourage you to honor your true spiritual nature. When you return to oneness, your spirit body will review all phases of your most recent life as well as all lifetimes. Your personality in your plane judges harshly, yet your spiritual nature knows you've received many teachings. Some need more rest than others before going on to their next assignment. The difficulty of the transition and the difficulty of the most recent life will determine the nature and length of your rest.

When you leave your world, your lifetime has come to completion. Yet that does not mean that your karmic cycles have come to completion. The accumulation of lifetimes will determine your completion of the earth cycles. Your spirit will decide and has already decided how to proceed.

Your spirit also develops and rejoices when you pay attention and honor your spirit while you're in physicality. Although death for many is a time of grief, your spiritual nature celebrates and rejoices. As one soul leaves, another one incarnates and the cycle begins again. The souls who are leaving will free energetic space for other light beings to come into the earth plane. And the ones who have recently left may be resting to gear up and return with glory.

Many of you are finishing your karmic cycles. With the increased energy and planetary shifts and the assistance of the angelic kingdom, your transformation is at hand. The awakened souls who have passed over are waiting in the wings for the right opportunity to come back and assist. Many, who worked so diligently at awakening others when they were in physicality, have had an opportunity to continue their work on our side. Yet many know returning as an ascended master will allow them to complete a higher assignment. The task of returning to physicality with universal knowledge and memory will escalate all souls paths on their way to oneness. Although in a physical body, the ascended masters are working on higher levels. They are empowering souls and raising the universal, cosmic and galactic vibrations in preparation for the next dimensional shift.

Although death is a trying time for the ones left without their physical friend, know that the ones who have transited are in grand preparation for their next assignment. They are the ones directly encouraging you to raise your vibrational levels. All those loved ones who pass over before you, are preparing space for you in the spirit plane and in your physical world.

Many parents wish to pass over before their child. Yet when the child goes first, know you have been blessed to have a special, wise soul whose tremendous light will carry you through your grief. They are the ones who will prepare the way for you. They have left their legacy with you and wish for your happy return to your spirit family. Although spirit families and physical families are not always the same, be assured, until the time comes for your transition, a member of your spirit family will be guiding you throughout your life.

The parent who passes over before the child is grown, leaves the child many gifts. Although the child may grieve, the parent leaves a knowing wisdom in the child about the return to Source. The spiritual parent is able to guide the child throughout the rest of his/her lifetime. The child may need time to realize the bond, but the spiritual connection between father and son or mother and daughter is never broken, but strengthened with time.

Finally, the departing of lovers, or husband and wife, is a physical separation only. Again, whichever one chooses to go first is paving the way for the other. As a twin flame or soul mate, the light of the one who has passed over will guide the earthbound one back home. The partner that goes first is teaching and encouraging the other one. Have you ever wondered why older adults die within six months of each other? Many times the brightness of the soul that departed first was needed to shed light and illuminate the final teachings of the one left. The older adults who have had an unshakeable bond continue to be guided by the other, their earthly work coming fast to completion. Transition allows them to reunite with each other.

We encourage you to grieve the loss of the physical relationship that comes with death, but in the same breath to rejoice for the freedom that the departed one now has. When you send affirming thoughts of embracing the light through prayer or meditation, your loved one moves through transition with joy and ease. We encourage you to move through your grief so the departed one may go on to embrace their next mission and celebrate living in the light.

The cycles of birth, life and death are inherent to your plane. The cycles help you to realize spiritual growth. Yet in our plane, cycles are not necessary and growth is a simultaneous event. We do not exist in a hierarchical world of comparison, "your spiritual growth is greater than mine." We exist in a state of oneness and harmony, embracing all the different souls with different missions, knowing we are all part of the same Source. We encourage you to look at your world through the eyes of oneness. Soon the demarcations of the cycles become less defined and an all-knowing of eternal existence is seen.

As with my brother-in-law, "Wills," fourteen years ago, I cried when Carol passed over. My tears were different this time. After experiencing the "other side," I now look at death as a transition. Carol had completed her work on earth and moved on with glory. Wills was in the spiritual planes of "winter," resting, gearing up for his next assignment. Byron and I welcomed the possibility of a child in our lives and embraced all the inherent challenges of parenting. Maybe the natural cycles of birth, life and death weren't so strange after all.

Epilogue

Spring 1996

Has a water glass ever exploded in your hand? I was surprised the first time it happened to me. The next day and the second glass that exploded, I understood.

After our journey to the Philippines, Byron and I consciously changed our lives. I aligned myself with my true spiritual nature and became an inspirational writer and lecturer. Byron reorganized his business and released his daily struggles. What we didn't understand was how much the universe was about to change our lives.

One night washing dishes at the kitchen sink, I turned to Byron and said, "We need a sign if we're to have a child." I picked up my glass of water and gestured upward with it. Within seconds, the glass shattered into tiny sharp pieces, neatly contained in the sink. I didn't get cut but jumped with surprise. "The universe works fast." But how could I be sure this was a sign. Although I didn't fear death, according to the "experts," I would be gambling my life away if I were to attempt a pregnancy.

The next evening while washing dishes, I marveled at the events of the previous night. I said to Byron, "Do you really think it's wise to take a chance? Am I well enough to carry a pregnancy without losing our child's life or my life?"

Byron said, "We are here because we've taken chances. I believe if this soul wants to come into our lives then both of you will survive. Maybe this pregnancy will be your ultimate healing." I gave Byron a questioning but loving look. He continued, "I support you with whatever decision you make. Ask the universe again if you need to know."

I lifted my glass, half in jest and said, "Okay, universe, if we're supposed to have a child, give me another sign." I felt energy rush into the top of my head and run through my left arm. The second glass exploded. I was a believer. I was healthy and well. This pregnancy would confirm my healing. I would remember this night whenever I feared adversity or lacked trust during my pregnancy. **Less than one year later, without complications, our son, Elijah Evans Martin was born.**

I am grateful for the abundance of love and guidance that continues to bless my life. The greatest gift of all is love - and the past five months "love" has infused our lives through the incarnation of our son. Every day I marvel at Elijah's growth and development. At his young age, he has already taught us that medical miracles and spiritual gifts are possible. Anything is possible with hope, faith and love. And, I'm astounded by the immeasurable amounts of joy he has brought into our lives. There are moments when I feel universal love permeate every fiber of my being so abundantly that I know beyond a doubt, I have found "Home - Home in the reflection of the light and love for another."

Addendum

Divine Order

During the process of this book, my editor, George, had a deep concern about using the terminology that "the world is in perfect order." He questioned the philosophy behind "perfection." On my manuscript, he wrote, "It's hard to believe that with all its tragedies, the world is absolutely perfect and needs no improvement."

With the evidence of so much chaos, suffering and hardship in the world, I've had these same questions. Why are children victims of hideous crimes? Why do people suffer with disease? During my health trials, I would often question the idea of "perfect divine order."

Guidance from the other side is not always what I want to hear. When I receive information, I ask for humility and reception, to bring forth messages with clarity and compassion. Understanding the information is an interpretation left to each one of us. And as my guides have said before, "If the words do not 'resonate' with you, then know they were not intended for you in this moment...glean what information you desire and leave the rest." With regards to **Divine Order**, the following information was given.

Divine Order

How can there be divine order with so much suffering in the world?

Divine order is a difficult concept for many to understand. The nature of free-will choice permits the atrocities which happen. You see, my children, in your world, things are not always what they appear to be.

Compassion is needed during this discussion - compassion for loved ones who witness darkness; compassion and gratitude for the "victim;" compassion for the perpetrator and compassion for your judgmental self. In your world, "victim" is a disempowering term. "Victim" implies a lack of understanding for the wisdom of that soul.

When a hideous crime is committed, it seems that darkness has prevailed. Yet, the only element that prevails with everlasting force is love. Fearing the world only perpetuates darkness. Darkness perpetuates criminal acts. The only way to coax the darkness into the light is through love.

An element of fear is attachment. Attachment to people and things is inherent to your world. We are not suggesting you stop feeling or caring about each other to free yourself from attachment. Instead, we encourage you to embrace your feeling state. When you experience the loss of a loved one through the chaotic world, we are here to tell you that their life was not wasted. Your loved one lived a purposeful life. Their passing was orchestrated beyond your conscious knowing.

What appears to be chaos and disorder to the earthly self is understood completely by the spiritual self. All souls are on a path of growth and learning. Many times the lessons learned or teachings taught are not easy ones.

Each soul has a divine purpose and there is divine order to that purpose. At a soul level, those who have taken on challenges such as disease, disability or abuse are your greatest teachers in physical form. They are your torch bearers, leaving their legacy and a gift for everyone they have touched.

Your soul is your supporting guardian and will guide you back home to oneness and divine unity. When you question your divinity, feel lost in the universe, or anger toward your creator, those are the times that you are being guided and supported the most. We will never leave you, especially in your time of greatest need. When you lack trust in the divine plan because you can't see the way, we are here to wipe off your windshield. Questioning is part of your nature and allows room for spiritual growth.

In a sea of unconditional love, our world is free of time, space, attachment and judgment. Divine love is in divine order. When we say "the world is in perfect order," we are looking at your world through the eyes of oneness. Your world is only a momentary moment. Striving, achieving and seeking only takes away from embracing the "All." Living moment-by-moment allows you to move into embracing the "Isness."

The earthly self, knowing physical pain and emotions, would not choose to subject oneself to disorder. Yet when viewed from oneness, there is perfect order in your world. Even the natural disasters such as earthquakes, hurricanes, and floods have their place.

With limited vision and three-dimensional blinders on, one cannot perceive the reason behind suffering. As we have said before, "Inherent to life itself is suffering. With suffering comes meaning and with meaning comes freedom." Meaning can only be found within each one of you.

We encourage you to go to your inner world. Is the outside world mirroring your inner recesses? Disorder inside appears as disorder outside. When there is love in your inner world, you reflect love to your outer world.

Souls do not choose to come into a life filled with hardship and abuse. They incarnate to learn and grow. Yet to learn and grow with joy and ease does not require striving or improving but "being." When you embrace your human-ness with all its "imperfections," then you are living in perfection. You see my children, by accepting yourself and the universe with all its "imperfections," you are then loving yourself more. The more you love yourself unconditionally, then the more you have room to love others. Embracing your humanness with all its "imperfections" puts change into motion without effort.

Contemplate for a moment how the world would change with the simple act of loving oneself completely and unconditionally. Abundant love would fill every crack and crevice of your being. Your glass would be full of love and overflow to others, leaving no room for fear or darkness. Your harmonious, peaceful world would be realized. When you can fully embrace life in the here and now with all its "imperfections," then you will see what a perfect moment of divine order you have just experienced in your world.

Acknowledgements

I'm happy to acknowledge those people who have lovingly impacted my life and thus this book. However, words hardly seem adequate to express the depths of my feelings. Therefore, as simple as the words sound, please know my love and gratitude are behind them.

First, I thank George Fisk, my editor. His guidance, thoughtful insight and friendship have not only enhanced this book but more importantly, my life. His enthusiasm never wavered and his understanding of my responsibilities as a new mother and a writer was more than anyone could ask for.

Many thanks to Dr. Kenneth Ring. I was honored, that with his schedule as a leader in the near-death research field, a pending book, a trip to Australia and deadlines for research, he still lovingly shared his precious time with me. As a fledgling in the literary world, he coached and encouraged me to finish my manuscript before the end of my pregnancy. Within one week of each other, the birth of my baby and the birth of this book took place.

I'm grateful to Mally Cox-Chapman for sharing her words of wisdom from her own experience as an author. Dr. Bruce Greyson, his wife Jenny and the Friends of IANDS Connecticut chapter have shown their continuous love and warmth. Thank you.

My heartfelt gratitude to all those mentioned in the text plus others who have inspired me along the way: Sherry Burns, Pat Campbell, Maureen Clinton, Beth deChamplain, Sandy Gourd, Nyla Hanson, Carol Howard, Nancy Dalmont Kruger, Jack Lardis, Susan LaRose, and Dennis Knapp, Connie Lussier, Anne Osiper, JoAnn Perry, Michael Phelan (my high school English tutor), Steve Price, Deirdre Robinson and Sally Weedon, Reva Seybolt, Al Sullivan, Greg Smiley, Larry and Martha Swan, Lisa Warren.

I'm grateful for the blending of allopathic and alternative medicine. I thank two outstanding health care professionals whose expertise came at critical times in my life: Dr. Tom Bell for giving me a second chance and Dr. Karen Green for guiding me through the miracle of birth.

Finally, my love and thanks to my supportive family throughout my lifetime: my grandparents Laurence and Erma Lougee; my parents Bob and Barbara Glass; my mother-in-law, Joy Logee Martin; my aunt Betsy Engvall and my uncle David Lougee; my other best friend and sister Ginger Castle and her husband Tobin; my three brothers Bob Jr., Jeffrey and Johnson Glass and their families; and my sister Gwendolyn Carbone and her husband Chuck, my godson Joseph Charles Carbone IV and my husband Byron Martin and our son Elijah.

Also, I acknowledge those who have gone before us. They continue to brighten the way for our happy and awaited return to the Light:

John Williams

Carol North

Ernest Martin

Doris Witter

Arthur and Evelyn Glass

Nanna Lougee

Grammie MacAllister